2879

D. Glen Aitken

THE JOY OF THE PLAIN LIFE

JOHN CHARLES COOPER

impact
books

Nashville, TN

THE JOY OF THE PLAIN LIFE © Copyright June 1981 by IMPACT BOOKS, a division of The Benson Company, Inc. All rights reserved. Printed in the United States of America. No part of this book may be used or reproduced in any manner whatsoever without written permission, except in the case of brief quotations embodied in critical articles and reviews. For information: IMPACT BOOKS, a division of The Benson Company, Inc., 365 Great Circle Road, Nashville, Tennessee 37228.

14015p
LC 81-47070
ISBN 0-914850-62-8

To the Poor of Asia and Latin America; the humble of Europe, Africa, and North America, with whom I have been privileged to visit on many a long walk under the burning sun and on many a cold and cloudy day.
God will fill you with good things in His own time. In the meantime, we who are fortunate must serve as His hands.

To the Poor in spirit, my parents, who made do, wore it out, ate it up, and generously shared with others and taught me to do the same.

And to my frugal wife, reared in the same tradition. The Lord gives in plenty; Man in his selfishness spurns plainness and creates poverty.

Forbid it, Lord that our roots become too firmly attached to this earth, that we should fall in love with things. Help us to understand that the pilgrimage of this life is but an introduction, a preface, a training school for what is to come.

Then shall we see all of life in its true perspective. Then shall we not fall in love with the things of time, but come to love the things that endure. Then shall we be saved from the tyranny of possessions which we have no leisure to enjoy, of property whose care becomes a burden. Give us, we pray, the courage to simplify our lives.

So help us, O God, to live and not merely to exist, that we may have joy . . .

Amen.
—PETER MARSHALL

The author and publisher express appreciation for the following materials:

Reprinted by permission of Harcourt Brace Jovanovich, Inc. from **Surprised By Joy** by C.S. Lewis Copyright 1955 by C.S. Lewis.

From **The Gospel of Luke,** Revised Edition, translated and interpreted by William Barclay. Copyright © 1975 by William Barclay. Published in the USA by The Westminster Press. Used by permission.

Used by permission of Bernard J. Topel.

Reprinted by permission of **Eternity** Magazine, Copyright 1980, Evangelical Ministries, Inc., 1716 Spruce Street, Philadelphia, PA 19103 (Dean Merrill, "Car Fever" September 1980).

Reprinted by permission of the author (David Breese, "Promises More Precious Than Gold" April 1980 **Moody Monthly**).

Reprinted by permission of the Ugandan Mission Committee from the March 1981 **Newsletter.**

Reprinted by permission of **Christianity Today** (Ronald J. Sider, "Cautions Against Ecclesiastical Elegance" copyright August 17, 1979).

Reprinted by permission of **United Evangelical Action,** the official publication of the National Association of Evangelicals (Alan Johnson, "Sin By Any Other Name . . ." Spring 1980).

Reprinted by permission of Schocken Books Inc. from **Living the Good Life: How to Live Sanely and Simply in a Troubled World** by Helen and Scott Nearing Copyright © 1954 by Helen Nearing.

Reprinted by permission of William B. Eerdmans Publishing Co. from **The Simple Life** by Vernard Eller Copyright © 1973.

Taken from **The Golden Cow** by John White. © 1979 by Inter-Varsity Christian Fellowship of the USA and used by permission of InterVarsity Press.

Taken from **Living More Simply,** ed. by Ronald J. Sider. © 1980 by Inter-Varsity Christian Fellowship of the USA and used by permission of InterVarsity Press.

Reprinted by permission of **Eternity** Magazine, Copyright 1979, Evangelical Ministries, Inc., 1716 Spruce Street, Philadelphia, PA 19103 (Lorry Lutz, "Credit Card Pilgrim" April 1979).

And for permission to quote Scripture passages from the following sources:

The **Revised Standard Version** of the Bible, copyrighted 1946, 1952, © 1971, 1973. Used by permission. Quoted verses are marked RSV.

The **Good News Bible,** the Bible in Today's English Version. Old Testament: Copyright © American Bible Society 1976; New Testament: Copyright © American Bible Society 1966, 1971, 1976. Used by permission. Quoted verses are marked GNB.

Holy Bible, New International Version, copyright © 1978, New York Bible Society. Used by permission. Quoted verses are marked NIV.

New American Standard Bible, copyright © The Lockman Foundation, 1960, 1962, 1963, 1972, 1973, 1975. Used by permission. Quoted verses are marked NASB.

CONTENTS

1 THE JOY OF THE NEW OBEDIENCE

The ground was frozen mud, petrified in awkward angles where the tracked vehicles had passed in warmer weather. Ungainly tents stood stark against a cold, black sky. I looked for stars but none were visible as I plodded toward a crazily-tilted tent standing at the edge of the encampment. Stooping to enter, I had to crawl inside over the straw-littered floor.

Perhaps a dozen Marines, dirty and cold, sat huddled together, seeking warmth in the straw and other human bodies. I burrowed in beside them. The temperature was forty degrees below zero. The First Marine Division had been locked in combat with Chinese Communist forces for the past month, and in the field against the North Koreans since September. Christmas Eve 1950 found my battalion safe at last, camped in an open field in South Korea. These bare quarters seemed the good life after weeks of danger and bitter cold.

An older man in the midst of the circle of youngsters gathered for Christmas services was a Lutheran chaplain. I recall little of the service that followed except that the chaplain prayed and delivered a brief sermon, and we all joined in singing hymns and carols. Yet I remember that evening as the occasion of the greatest joy I've ever experienced. For about a half hour I knew ultimate bliss. I was out of myself—although I remained cold, hungry, and tired to the point of exhaustion. Nonetheless, the songs, prayers, and familiar story of the birth of Jesus Christ, which I had known from childhood, came to life in that cold tent. I not only heard, I saw; moreover, I *experienced* that story for myself. Christ was born in me. I knew the joy that surpasses happiness and the peace that passes all understanding.

Many times since, surfeited with rich food and showered with fine presents, I have felt the real meaning of Christmas lacking in our celebration. Yet in that earlier time of want, I wanted for nothing. Without gift or banquet, I had all I needed. There was no feeling of depressive letdown that so often accompanies Christmas. Having nothing, I had everything. Tears rolled down my cheeks. I silently thanked God for delivering me from the terror and death of the past weeks. I quietly embraced the Lamb of God that takes away the sins of the world. Having nothing Himself, that Baby, born in a barn, reached into that stable-like tent and gave me Himself. I was rich in joy.

The Adventure of The Christian Life

Interestingly, my experience turned out to be a normal introduction to the Christian life, as I found later in my seminary studies. The joy that comes from knowing Christ is not a materialistic pleasure, a hail-fellow-well-met life of getting and having, but is more in the nature of an adventure, a real struggle, with the forces of the world pulling us this way and that. Oddly, it is not in having and possessing, but in giving and suffering that our justification by faith alone deepens into a life of new obedience in which we are conformed more and more to the image of Christ by the work of the Holy Spirit.

St. Francis of Assisi, a carefree young man of wealth, was converted to preaching the gospel in utter poverty through an illness. In a vision, the words of Matthew 10:7-10 became his personal command:

> "And preach as you go, saying, 'The kingdom of heaven is at hand!' Heal the sick, raise the dead, cleanse lepers, cast out demons. You received without paying, give without pay. Take no gold, nor silver, nor copper in your belts, no bag for your journey, nor two tunics, nor sandals, nor a staff; for the laborer deserves his food."
>
> (RSV)

Although his proud father was angry, Francis was true to the inner vision, and gave all his goods freely to the poor. Leaving home wearing rags and a rope belt, taken from a scarecrow, he wandered over the land, preaching and giving friendship to all. The order founded by Francis ministered especially to the poor and sick.

Just before his death, despite illness, pain, and even blindness, he composed the beautiful and spiritual "Canticle to the Sun." The joyfulness of Francis, in the midst of suffering while giving his all to others, makes him one of the most Christlike people who ever lived. As Francis prayed:

> Oh! Divine Master, grant that I may not so much seek to be consoled, as to console,
> Not so much to be understood as to understand;
> Not so much to be loved as to love;
> For it is in giving that we receive;
> It is in pardoning that we are pardoned;
> It is in dying that we awaken to eternal life.

Francis' life shows us the lesson I had to learn—and am still learning—after my Christmas Eve experience: there is joy in obedience to Jesus Christ. Once we stumble across the real meaning of joy, the world opens up for us. We see this lesson taught everywhere: in nature and poetry, in history and experience—and above all, in Scripture. Joy is participation in the work of Christ who is even now subduing the powers of this world unto Himself.

The famous missionary to the lepers, Father Damien, illustrates once more the joy that comes in the midst of the greatest difficulties—in the plainest, even most dangerous, of lives. Damien, who felt keenly God's call to show Christ's love to the outcasts of the leper colonies, served them so long and so intimately that he, too, contracted the disease. One morning during prayers he began his meditation by saying: "We lepers . . ."

One senses that he was filled with *joy* over being *one* with his people when he uttered those simple words. With the Apostle Paul, sincere Christians of every age can say humbly:

> Not that I complain of want; for I have learned, in whatever state I am, to be content. I know how to be abased, and I know how to abound; in any and all circumstances I have learned the secret of facing plenty and hunger, abundance and want. I can do all things in him who strengthens me.
>
> (Phil. 4:11-13 RSV)

It is precisely to help us enter into this "secret" of St. Paul, into this joy that far surpasses abundance or self-elected poverty, that this book is written.

Invitation to Joy

But "secrets" are never easy to discover. Indeed, the secrets of the Christian life can *never* be discovered through our own intellect and power. They are always surprises, experiences of insight and ecstasy that discover *us*. We do not find God and His gifts. He finds us.

We cannot strip ourselves of worldly anxieties and possessions and expect to have peace and joy. God must inspire and empower us to begin a simpler, plainer, more Christlike life—which culminates in joy.

C. S. Lewis in his book, *Surprised by Joy,* defines the end of our quest which he refers to as:

> an unsatisfied desire which is itself more desirable than any other satisfaction. I call it Joy, which is here a technical term and must be sharply distinguished both from Happiness and from Pleasure. Joy (in my sense) has indeed one characteristic, and one only, in common with them; the fact that anyone who has experienced it will want it again. Apart from that, and considered only in its quality, it might almost equally well be called a particular kind of unhappiness or grief. But then it is a kind we want. I doubt whether anyone who has tasted it would ever, if both were in his power, exchange it for all the pleasures in the world. But then Joy is never in our power and pleasure often is.

Lewis sees joy, too, as mingled with—perhaps growing out of—suffering. It is like the ecstasy that surges through a mountain climber, who has reached the top of a high peak only after hours of cruel and fatiguing hiking; or the exhilaration of the long-distance runner when, having driven his body past the point of near-exhaustion, he crosses to the finish line.

Yet joy in the Lord is never a human achievement. It comes to us in moments of stress and need as a free gift from God. As Martin Luther observes:

> I believe that I cannot by my own reason or strength believe in Jesus Christ my Lord, or come to Him; but the Holy Ghost has called me by the Gospel, enlightened me with His gifts, sanctified and kept me in the true faith . . .

All Christians are "surprised by joy," whether it is at conversion or while struggling through the complexities of the world, in war or peace, at school or work.

The great mathematician Blaise Pascal (1623-62), one of Europe's greatest intellects, wrote that God can only be known through Jesus Christ by an act of faith, itself given by God. Man's need for God is made evident, Pascal said, by man's misery apart from his Lord. Yet there is a vast distance between *knowing* God and *loving* Him. Loving joy in God is the essence of true faith, for the heart has reasons unknown to the mind.

It is said that Pascal's life was transfigured by an intense sense of Christ's presence:

Fire!

"God of Abraham, God of Isaac, God of Jacob," not of philosophers and scholars.
. . .
God of Jesus Christ.

A strong tradition tells us that Pascal wrote these words on a paper, which was found pinned to his inner shirt after his death.

Fire! Joy! Called by the Holy Spirit! Surprised! Transported beyond ourselves while still cold and covered with the filth of months of hard fighting—the dried blood of our friends stiff on our fatigues. Joy. The joy of being indwelt by the living presence of Christ. Once we have experienced that joy, we can only turn again to the anxious, confused world and, converted ourselves, tell our brothers and sisters. We are called to a life like His, a life that befits daily repentance and faith. Today, such a life must, of necessity, be a simpler, plainer life.

Seeing More Clearly

The nineteenth-century philosopher-naturalist, Henry David Thoreau, explaining his reasons for moving from town to Walden Pond said:

I went to the woods because I wished to live deliberately, to front only the essential facts of life, and see if I could not learn what it had to teach, and not, when I came to die, discover that I had not lived.

Like the hermits of the early Christian centuries, Thoreau

wished to clear his life of the clutter of the city. He wanted to commune with his own spirit and discover the inner vision. It's not surprising that Thoreau took many spiritual books with him. Among our contemporaries, there are those who attempt to imitate Thoreau. These folks, from ex-stockbrokers to dropped-out college students, are seeking to escape the rat race of modern city life. This is understandable, even admirable, but the desire to find peace of mind, or even to share more of our scarce natural resources with others, is not the full story of the committed Christian's search for joy in a plainer life.

Closer to the Christian motive, and perhaps a sterling example of the genuine search, is the story of Bishop Topel.

The Right Reverend Bernard J. Topel, Roman Catholic Bishop of Spokane, Washington, sold his mansion and chauffeur-driven car. He purchased an old home in a decaying neighborhood and a ten-year-old car he drives himself, giving the bulk of the money realized to the poor. Bishop Topel now raises his own food, and has spent nothing on groceries since January 1972. He voluntarily became a poor man, to help other people out of the poverty his station did not dictate.

While he does not elaborate, it is clear that the good Bishop is seeking to conform his life to that of the Ultimate Plain Man, who pronounced blessing upon the poor in spirit. When Jesus taught his disciples in the Sermon on the Mount that they were to discover poverty of spirit and be blessed (Matt. 5:3), He was suggesting that true joy or blessedness begins with an acknowledgment of spiritual poverty (bankruptcy) before God. This is the position of the Christian who depends on the daily indwelling of the Spirit for his spiritual sustenance. As faith is vitalized, this position of spiritual poverty may also lead to mental, emotional, and even physical poverty. We may admire Thoreau for wanting to experience the basic joys of self-imposed simplicity of life. But as followers of Jesus Christ we, like Bishop Topel, must strive to personalize His model of joyful suffering, as we are led by His Spirit.

The Ultimate Plain Person

Jesus came by His plainness—and the ecstatic joy of hard labor in God's service—naturally. Born while his humble peasant parents were far from home, forced by a military occupation's officials to register at their tribal seat, Jesus' birth was either in a cave or in a borrowed stable.

We are touched by what William Barclay refers to in his *The Gospel of Luke* as:

> the rough simplicity of the birth of the Son of God. We might have expected that, if he had to be born into this world at all, it would be in a palace or a mansion. There was a European monarch who worried his court by often disappearing and walking incognito amongst his people. When he was asked not to do so for security's sake, he answered, "I cannot rule my people unless I know how they live." It is the great thought of the Christian faith that we have a God who knows the life we live because he too lived it and claimed no special advantage over common men . . .
>
> It was into an ordinary home that Jesus was born, a home where there were no luxuries, a home where every penny had to be looked at twice, a home where the members of the family knew all about the difficulties of making a living and the haunting insecurity of life. When Life is worrying for us, we must remember that Jesus knew what the difficulties of making ends meet can be.

Reared as a Son of the Torah and as an apprentice carpenter to Joseph, his education was that of the Bar-mitzvahed Hebrew boy! He could read the sacred scrolls. Later Jesus' Pharisaic adversaries expressed amazement that He knew the Hebrew alphabet at all.

After his call to the Messianic task and His baptism by His cousin John, Jesus led the life of an itinerant preacher. He seems to have owned nothing but the clothes on His back. His food and lodging were provided by those, like Mary and Martha, to whom He ministered. More often, He slept by the roadside (as I have often done in my travels), wrapping up in His robe and lying down on the bare ground, accepting whatever the elements might bring.

But Jesus was no ascetic. His friends included both the outcasts and the elite of His society. He did not shun social gatherings or decline occasional comforts. He dined with the wealthy, attending weddings and feasts. Jesus' commitment was to the devastating, damnable spiritual void in people with hurts—whoever they might be. His compassion blinded him to creed or color or bank account. Yet His *detachment* from material bondage was total and perfect. Our weakness demands His lordship and leadership in discovering our personal position in regard to material wealth.

It is true that Jesus was the special friend of the poor, of the dispossessed, of those a modern Algerian writer has called "the wretched of the Earth." Many members of this fold seem to have followed Him from place to place. Those who were outcast because of leprosy or life style or morals were befriended by Him. Jesus' only harsh words were for the powerful, the unjust, and the hypocritical. These powerful upholders of the *status quo* in religion and state brought about His death.

As the world knows, Jesus was abandoned by *all* men, betrayed, and cruelly put to death in the manner reserved for rebellious slaves. His body was recovered by friends and laid in a tomb belonging to someone else. If God had not raised Him from the dead and proclaimed Him the Christ, the Son of God, His name might have disappeared from the memory of man.

Yet, in a way greater even than St. Paul realized, Jesus counted it all joy, even the cross that was set before Him. Why? For He was one with God. This is the One who calls us to the joy of the plain life, taking up our cross to follow Him, entering the narrow door that leads to life in its fullness, and turning away from the broad path that leads to anxiety and self-defeat.

Life Outside the Fast Lane

Those wide paths may be understood as wrong turnings to

either the left or the right, away from the narrow road of plainness that involves living in the present (yet future) kingdom of God. As Luther reminds us, the kingdom of God is not a place but is wherever and whenever the will of God is done. Life in the new obedience, which begins with our justification of faith, through grace, for Christ's sake, goes on through all our days and years. The new obedience starts when we are saved and is a continual process of sanctification through life. Since santification means becoming more and more like Christ, it surely will mean a weaning away from *emphasis on* and *bondage to* material possessions and power. How else could we be growing into the image of One who freely laid aside His likeness with God and became a Poor Man in spirit and fact, with no place to lay His head? (Phil. 2:5-11)

Contrasted to life on the narrow path, there is the wide path of affluence, power, and wealth that so many North American Christians now follow. This is "life in the fast lane," filled with activities and things. Jesus' parable of the thorns and weeds that spring up to choke out the spiritual life is very appropriate. We all experience the weeds of demands upon our time, the desire to take part in more and more social activities, hobbies, parties, or to work overtime or "moonlight." Soon we become enslaved to these activities and desires, thinking that we must milk every moment of pleasure, every opportunity of financial or social profit. We begin to believe this physical life is all the life there is. At that point, not only weeds and thorns, but the deadly nightshade, the intoxicating weeds of darkness, smother our souls.

The results are familiar to many in our society: fatigue, both mental and physical; spiritual drifting; loneliness; tension; anxiety; and, ultimately, depression. This spiritual disease of materialism with its accompanying devastating consequences is the motivation for many who are seeking a simpler life. Yet even these may be disappointed in their quest. Merely leaving high-pressure jobs and the social whirl will not bring joy.

There are those who may miss the joy of kingdom-living in another direction, also. Not only wealth, but the lack of wealth, can produce identical symptoms of distress. Those who sit on the fringes of affluency may be eaten up with envy for those who are mistakenly believed to ''have it made.'' The feeling of being cut off from the fast lane leading to the middle and upper classes often breeds anger and rebellion. Though the poor of our rural slums and inner cities are frequently the downtrodden, oppression doesn't automatically create saints. More often, it causes hostility, erupting in violence, or low self-esteem, resulting in stagnation and apathy.

The end result of either extreme—miserable rich or miserable poor—is death, and both are bound together in their self-destruction. But it should not be so for the Christian!

Spiritual Poverty

For those who know Christ, entering upon the life of new obedience means beginning to grow in meekness, poverty of spirit, mercy, love, and righteous conduct. The new obedience demands a spirit of plainness in the inner person. We will feel moved to love (not merely to give token expressions of charity) because Christ first loved us. We will recognize the present and future existence of God's kingdom as the living Christ moves and motivates the members of His body. We can find the strength and courage to live without dependence upon things and money only if we are in daily, deepening communion with Christ and others in the community of faith.

There is a joy that surpasses the pride and smugness of material possessions. It is the joy of following Christ, for the essence of the simpler life lies in its Christlikeness, the casting away of extra coats and the burden of ''things''—so as to step out cleanly into the future, wearing the amazingly light yoke of loving service to others.

Only when we are conformed more closely to the image of Christ will we truly become poor in spirit and, looking upon those less fortunate than ourselves, make the decision to share—of ourselves, our earthly goods, and our Lord. Then we may bring to Bishop Topel's example a new dimension, alive with meaning for our personal lives.

LIVING THE JOY

Bishop Bernard J. Topel

In 1974, several years before major energy cutbacks were requested of the American people at large, Bishop Bernard J. Topel, of Spokane, Washington, had set the temperature in his modest four-room frame house at a chilly forty degrees.

The Most Reverend Bishop Topel, from 1966-1978 the Roman Catholic Bishop of Spokane and spiritual leader of a 74,000-member diocese, had chosen to ignore the directive expressed in a letter written to him by one of his critics: "Kings should live like kings, princes should live like princes, and bishops should live like bishops."

"Should Bishops Live Like Bishops?"

Instead of a sumptuously furnished mansion, the Bishop chose for his dwelling an ill-repaired cottage in a blue-collar neighborhood. The house cost $4000 in 1970, perhaps because of the previous owner's difficulty in getting paint to stay on it. Four years after moving in, the Bishop was rewarded with a paint job, carried out by volunteer members of his flock.

"I have come to the realization," the bishop mildly explains, "that the most important thing I can do in the church, and that applies to Christians in general, is to live simply in order to give money to the poor."

The Bishop certainly never could be accused of lavish spending for food. In the years between 1973 and 1978, he paid not one cent for the food he consumed. Beginning with a single packet of seeds, the Bishop now lays claim to row upon row of vegetables—beans, peas, carrots, lettuce, and the more exotic Jerusalem artichokes and comfrey (an herb used mainly for tea).

The Bishop does not vary his frugal diet even for guests. A visitor was given his choice of fish-head or lentil soup, followed by a salad of homegrown lettuce with a dressing of dill-pickle juice, and topped off with a dessert of neighbor-donated rolls, to which Bishop Topel added homegrown rhubarb.

Belt-Tightening As A Way of Life

Not only does he tighten his belt in an effort to conserve food, the Bishop often must tighten the belt on a pair of too-large, worn-out trousers, with patches ironed on their threadbare knees. His over-sized black shoes, bequeathed to him by a fellow priest who died several years ago, are made the right size by wearing a couple of pairs of socks. The extra socks are a help, though, in combating the cold temperatures inside his house, and he also wears coat, hat, and muffler indoors. His perpetually chilly state moved a sympathetic Jewish matron in faraway New York to send a donation of thermal underwear and ski socks, gratefully accepted by the Bishop after he had pointed out to her that needy persons must exist in her own city.

Thieves Escape With Solitary Dollar

Ridiculous as it may seem, thieves did attempt to rob the Bishop some time ago, breaking in through the back door, now patched with plywood. They were lucky enough to find the dollar that he had put aside for seeds for his garden, for that was the only money (or indeed, anything of value) in the house.

Though vows of poverty are not exactly new to the religious world, the Bishop seems to take his beyond the normal limits imposed upon a churchman of his standing.

Overall, though the number of dollars he has been able to save by strict adherence to his self-imposed poverty will certainly never wipe out the suffering and deprivation of the poor, he does not feel that is what matters.

**Value of Simple
Living Is In
Sharing**

For Bishop Topel, and by implication for all other Christians, the joy of living modestly is in sharing with those who have even less. He puts himself on their level because those who come to him for help "are much more at home in my little house than they would be in a stately residence."

Bishop Topel, retired since late 1978, continues to live simply in Spokane, ministering to the city's poor. Portions of this account originally appeared in Time *magazine November 13, 1978.*

THE JOY OF LETTING GO

Quietly enjoying a walk along the beach, the young man's reverie is suddenly shattered by a woman's shrill cry.

"Save me! I'm drowning!"

Looking out at the breaking waves, he spies a floundering figure. Almost without thought, he races into the surf and begins taking long strokes into the deeper water. Reaching the thrashing woman, he clasps her around the waist.

"Be calm! Be calm!" he whispers hoarsely.

But the woman is in panic and wraps her arms around his head and neck, pulling the rescuer under. The man struggles to free himself, shouting, "You have to let go! Let go! You can't be saved if you don't let go!"

Robert Frost once wrote about the plain and simple joys of swinging in tree branches, saying it was good to swing in branches, both coming and going. Letting go, removing ourselves from the economic and social race for supremacy that for so long has characterized the West, is good both in extracting ourselves from the expected pattern and in finding ourselves in possession of new freedoms.

The Great American Nightmare

Yet a few years ago the idea of urging people to adopt a plainer, simpler life style would have been considered absurd. After World War II had stimulated the American economy and laid the Great Depression to rest, the American dream began to be a reality for millions of families. There was work for most at good pay. Credit was easy to obtain and people began to buy their own homes, drive their own cars, and take expensive vacations. The prevailing philosophy was "bigger and better."

That philosophy wasn't difficult to accept. The GI Bill funneled millions of veterans into college and vocational schools; and the continuing Cold War, with periodic flare-ups in Korea and Southeast Asia, fueled the economy to offset occasional downswings in the business cycle. Gasoline cost thirty cents a gallon, the U.S. inflation rate was the lowest in the industrialized world, and Americans considered themselves very lucky!

Since the Vietnam War, the OPEC decision to use oil as a weapon, and the growing public awareness that the world's natural resources are being consumed at phenomenal rates, our economic, military, and political positions as a world power have gradually reversed. Now the price of gasoline exceeds by more than a dollar a gallon the price in those earlier days. American power is flouted in some countries, ignored by others, and generally questioned around the world. After several years of double-digit inflation, the "American dream" contains nightmarish qualities.

Against this background of dysfunction and distress, the urgency and popularity of a plainer life style is upon us.

The Plain Life Defined

But just what is "the plain life?" The plain life is but one term referring to a new—yet older—manner of living. In my book *Finding a Simpler Life,* written in 1974, I called the life style "simple" merely to coin a new phrase for what Helen and Scott Nearing had called "the good life." Others undoubtedly consider this growing social movement as a means of restoring the life style of their youth or to returning nostalgically to the less complex society of their parents and grandparents—a renaissance of "the good old days." By our definition, however, plain living aims at freedom from the bonds of our complex, interdependent society by *modesty of life* and the *discipline of our acquisitive desires.*

One hundred and fifty years ago, our ancestors staked their claim to the New Land, living on isolated farms spread out all over the North American continent. Life was hard, then, but satisfying and singularly free of stress. Today, our lives generally lack the necessity of hard manual labor, but paradoxically, they are filled with anxieties, stress, and fear. The complexities of our lives and interdependencies that make our physical existence easier also contribute to tensions, red tape, and interpersonal conflicts. As these tensions accelerate, many are seeking ways to escape the undesirable side effects of our stressful age. Both within and outside the church, the peaceful joys of a plainer life are more and more often the subject of discussion.

Modesty of Life

A few years ago, a movie entitled *Network* presented a TV news commentator who started a people's revolt with the slogan "I'm mad . . . and I'm not going to take it anymore."

Over the past two decades, numerous Americans, not so much mad as fed up, have decided not to take it anymore and have begun to untangle themselves from the golden cords of luxury, overconsumption, and materialism. They have struck out in many directions. The hippie youth movement, the peace movements, and the civil rights movements of several years ago, as well as the ecology and physical fitness advocates of more recent times, make clear the widespread recognition that something is wrong with America. These attempts to bring solution to the problems are commendable, but inadequate.

Something more basic is breaking the heart of America. It is the ignorance of or willful disregard for some words spoken from a mountainside nearly two thousand years ago: "Seek ye first the kingdom of God and His righteousness; and all these things shall be added unto you" (Matt. 6:33). We have it all wrong—precisely backwards. It is time we set our priorities straight. Once we have aligned ourselves with God's plan, we may find partial answers in the rediscovery of thrift and frugality.

Two Motivations for Thrift

Thrift is not a new concept in Western society. Our ancestors were thrifty people because they had to be. "Eat it up. Wear it out. Make it do, or do without" was the motto of the majority of families until a very few years ago. Certainly the extremist—the tight-fisted miser, the Ebenezer Scrooge type—is hardly a Christian concept.

But there was another style of thrift in the past that was and is distinctly Christlike. John Wesley, the famous father of Methodism, taught his early followers to "earn all you can, save all you can, give all you can." His interpretation of plain living was to secure goods and materials *for the purpose of helping others*.

Not long ago a friend of mine told me about a Korean gentleman who had come to this country and prospered. In an example of the kind of spiritual thriftiness we are advocating, this gentleman and his wife, upon reaching retirement age, adopted a Central American girl. Though he found it necessary to return to work to support his enlarged family, his statement was beautifully simple and selfless. "I believe in investing in people, not in things," he firmly emphasizes.

A Christian life of modesty does no[t]
work and compensation for work. But if we
over goods, materials, and possessions, our p
must be in people and in service.

The Discipline of Our Acquisitive Desires

On every hand we are bombarded by sights and sounds th[at]
out *Buy! Buy!* Turn on the TV—and commercials, three at a ti[me]
blast off every twelve minutes. Turn on the radio—and salesmen
hawking their wares, outshout the singers, belting out popular
songs. Open a magazine—and attractive models, both male and
female, languish seductively against automobiles, liquor bottles,
and refrigerators. Their message: You are what you buy! How are
we, then, to discipline lifelong habits of acquisitive desires, rein-
forced by the materialistic culture in which we live?

The habit can be broken only by a new focus, inspired and
encouraged by the indwelling Spirit of God. As St. Augustine,
the early church father, observed: We are guided in life by what
we love. If we love the things that money can buy, we will be
guided, even driven, by the desire to accumulate things. If we
love God, the Source of all good, we will be guided by the desire
to serve and please Him. The discipline of our desire to acquire
material possessions, then, grows out of our communion with
God through Christ. We really need to change our heads and
hearts before we can hope to change our habits.

Based on this new focus, the believer needs to develop
counter-habits. Guided by the Holy Spirit, we can:

1. Cultivate an attitude of aloofness toward advertising. It may
even be necessary to turn off the television and radio during
commercials, to cancel subscriptions to magazines heavily en-
dorsed by consumer-oriented advertising, and to skip over the
sections of the newspapers saturated with attractive sales pitches
from local stores.

2. Reassess what we already own, asking ourselves the hard

...essary? We may discover
...own us.

...our material possessions
...The American dream is
...with the Joneses" is a
...ourselves by the wrong
... status are real tempta-
...

...l., writes in a letter to

...ount of money would be released for
...strategic causes if Christians *en masse* would live aloof from
peer pressure and compulsive advertising and would resist buying
things just because they have money.

We do need to change our ways of dealing with things, but we
also need to change our attitudes toward that other gift of God,
time itself.

Redeeming the Time

Whenever two people meet today, one or the other is sure to
mention how busy he or she is; no one seems to have any free
time. And though we may not know exactly where we are going,
most of us are racing the clock to get there!

In an effort to endure the fast, meaningless pace of our lives,
vast quantities of alcohol, tobacco, marijuana, and other legal
and illegal drugs are consumed by our population. This futile
attempt is merely a reflection of the enormous changes taking
place constantly in our culture.

Alvin Toffler has written in his book *Future Shock* of the
culmination of rapidly accelerating technological changes since
the beginning of the century. In seventy years, he reminds us, we
have moved from the Wright Brothers' aircraft (little more than a
powered kite) to the Concorde, flying more than twice the speed
of sound, to rockets that have placed man on the moon.

Rapid Western and Japanese technological advances have depleted materials and energy at such alarming rates that the world faces the imminent exhaustion of petroleum and other vital mineral reserves. Not one of us—faced with higher gasoline prices and a lower speed limit—is unaware of the damage done to our culture by the sophisticated, consumptive life style of the past seventy-five years.

With the onset of higher fuel prices, the inflationary processes already at work in this country have escalated. Life has become harder for persons in the lower- and middle-income brackets. For the very poor, the elderly and the retired—all those on fixed incomes—the outlook is bleak, indeed. It has become increasingly difficult to eat well and keep warm in the winter—and for some, it is literally a matter of life and death.

Inflation, itself a result of our stressful, quickly obsolescent life styles, is in turn creating even more stress. Under such conditions, something must break—and all too often it is the hearts and the minds of our people.

Into our distress as we race headlong toward oblivion comes a still, small voice: " 'Come to me, all you who are weary and burdened, and I will give you rest . . . For my yoke is easy and my burden is light' " (Matt. 11:28,30 NIV). Simplifying inevitably leads to a calmer, more tranquil state. We can begin to perceive a way out of our confusion.

Some years ago I wrote a poem in an attempt to translate what an old Korean man had said during the 1950-53 war, about the huge spotlights and searchlights mounted on the front lines. These thousands-of-candle-watt lights were used to blind and illuminate the Chinese Communist troops as they attempted to crawl forward to our trenches and bunkers dug into the sides and tops of hills along the Thirty-Eighth Parallel. Sometimes the lights, mounted on trucks or small platforms with wheels, would reveal hundreds of enemy soldiers, weapons in hand, running straight toward our trenches. The shouting and bugle-blowing, the deafening noise of the machine guns, and the weird, ear-splitting sound of whistles blown by the Chinese officers leading the attack are forever emblazoned in my mind in a scene out of Dante's *Inferno*. The lights, literally making day out of night, made it possible for us to stop these wild charges even though we were outnumbered many times over. Looking on in amazement, the old gentleman said:

> You have forgotten the truth about time,
> You have broken the cycle of work and rest,
> You have lit an imaginary sun
> And raped the night,
> Stealing away her healing powers.
> If your tomorrow is not good,
> It will only be
> Because you have robbed tomorrow
> For the sake of today.

What that wise man said in war is also true in time of peace in technologically developed countries. Our lives are out of sync with the cycles of nature. We must remember how to rest and in whom to rest.

Return to Paradise?

For the plain person, nature symbolizes the processes of life. We know that nature is created by God, but we also know that it can be a crucible in which man degrades himself. Nature is the arena of our activities, and what we do to nature, we do directly to ourselves.

There is a natural cycle to every day, to every month, and to every life: the cycle of the sun—rise, advance, decline, and set; the movement of the moon through its periods; the expansion and contraction of natural energy; and the progression of life, from birth to maturity to old age and death. These processes validate themselves because they are elements of nature.

Living in conscious harmony with nature—and we all live unconsciously bound to these processes without reflection or effort—is deeply and finally satisfying. For day, night, month, and life are the structures of our very being itself. When life in the modern world is experienced as a state of deprivation, anxiety, and despair, it is because the structures man has erected for himself are often cerebral and thus, partially or wholly artificial.

An electric light excuses us from observing the changing pattern of light and dark during a twenty-four-hour period. Air conditioning removes us from the warmth of midday and the cool of evening. Industrial pollution separates us from invigorating fresh air and clean skies. Patterns of work, geared to the production and consumption of goods and services that separate us from nature, make man stronger into the world that has produced him.

When we get away from the city to the undeveloped areas in our country, we begin to realize that, in the city, we have lost our true home. For thousands of years, civilization has sought to remove man from a passive role as part of the world and make him master of the world. Twentieth-century man has simply completed the process.

Urban Pioneers

The twentieth century has become a kind of prison of artificial existence for those of us who live in the technologically wealthy West. We are held willingly, without real freedom or true enjoyment, because we are spoiled by the luxury of modern conveniences. Many of us are content to live these soft lives. But among others there stirs a feeling of uneasiness, of lost pleasures, of loneliness in the midst of crowds, and above all, of a sense of death in the midst of that genuine life that still goes on all around us in the natural kingdoms of grasses, birds, and animals.

Over the years, since World War II, literally millions of Americans and Canadians on this great North American continent have been drawn from the large cities. They had moved to those urban areas originally seeking upward mobility, more money and power.

Subsequently, there have been seasonal out-migrations accomplished with the aid of tents and trailers, motor homes, and campers. National and state parks have been overcrowded, and the great North-South interstate highways choked to a standstill by the tourists and winter "snowbirds" fleeing the North for the warmer South. Camping became a way of life—at least until the energy crisis struck. These people were seeking an escape from the artificiality of human relations in the business and social worlds of modern North America. They were seeking, like modern-day Thoreaus, to remove themselves from the cities, those great pleasure palaces that had become prisons.

Some people, still drawn to what remains of unspoiled nature, have moved to the mountains of Colorado or the woods of Maine. Communes have sprung up in abundance in Vermont and Arizona. But it is not necessary to flee the city and hide in the woods to reestablish contact with nature.

Human beings can discipline their actions. We can rise earlier and go to bed earlier. We can cultivate green things, raising food as well as flowers, even in the tiniest garden plot in the city. We can seek our recreation in parks, on long walks, in jogging or riding bicycles, instead of in passive spectator sports or riding in cars.

Today, the outward migration from cities to suburbs and small towns is reversing. People are returning to the center cities because of opportunities for cheaper housing, mass transit, and proximity to places of work. Why cannot these new "urban homesteaders" try to humanize and "naturalize" the asphalt jungle of the inner city?

In the heart of downtown Helsinki, we find apartment buildings surrounded by parks and trees and ponds. The city can be reclaimed for humane living. Perhaps it will be, if Christians show the way.

Coming Out

Around the time of the British Reformation of the sixteenth century, there were a number of lay-oriented religious movements. John Wycliffe, the "Morning Star of the Reformation," who translated the Scriptures from Latin to English so that "every plowboy could read the Bible in his native tongue," was also the father of a lay-preaching movement.

These lay preachers preached the gospel, but also a kind of "come out from among them and be separate" sectarianism that included the rejection of all modern developments. In particular, this group wished to smash the machinery of the developing water-operated mills and spinning wheels. In time they came to be called "Levellers" and their preachers the "Lollards." This name derived from the fact that they "lolly-gagged" around talking instead of working as good peasants should.

The name "Lollards" has now become a synonym for all those who wish to turn back from the mechanical, technological developments of society. Until just recently, the Lollards were decried and made the butt of historians' jokes. Now many of us are beginning to feel that we at least know how they must have felt. When faced with the prospect of losing personal identity other than a number in a computer, many people are out-and-out Lollards today.

Somewhere, somehow, sometime—many of us want to break free from the tyranny of numbers, of computerized society, and return to the freedom of non-regulation, into the joy of non-recognition, to the private, basic, plainer, numberless life.

Letting Go

In the final analysis, the Christian's plain philosophy is a call to the life style of Christ. It is a call to what was termed, in the Middle Ages, a sacramental life style. This way of living is in harmony with one another and with nature.

As I contemplate the joy that can come when our nervous energies are freed up to engage in meaningful communion with God and His creation, I feel moved to strip down to basics in my life.

During my service in the Korean Conflict, I recall troops setting out on the march, burdened down with every possible creature comfort. After about a dozen miles on foot, the line of march began to be littered with unnecessary items that had been discarded. Even extra food was thrown away as backs and legs grew stiff from exertion. I recall dropping most of the Christmas gifts I had received in mail call immediately before this long, thirty-five-mile march. It hurt to leave behind a new comb and brush set, books, and other special things sent to me by my family at home. But there were many miles to go and dangers that would require all my energies.

Just before reaching the Secondary Line of Resistance behind the Main Line of Resistance, each man dropped his entire pack, keeping only a little food rolled in a poncho and a pair of socks stuffed in a pocket.

In order to run forward and gain the victory, in battle or in life, we must "lay aside every weight, and sin which clings so closely . . . For the moment all discipline seems painful rather than pleasant; later it yields the peaceful fruit of righteousness to those who have been trained" (Heb. 12:1, 11 RSV).

LIVING THE JOY

Russ Flint

It all began with a plate of spaghetti. I stared at the steaming dish that my wife, Cheryl, had placed on the table and asked,

"What about the *Reader's Digest* article?"

"Which article?"

"The one that said that all commercial pastas are just empty calories and empty bulk."

"But I know you like spaghetti," she said. "I thought once in a while would be all right."

To that, I raised my forefinger and wagged it with great resolve, "If spaghetti is nothing but empty calories, *let's not eat it!*"

**Spaghetti Just
The Start**

It was the spaghetti decision that led to me quit my job, sell our possessions, including house and car, take three of our four children out of school, and buy an old pickup and a twenty-one-foot travel trailer, which would be our home while we looked for acreage in northern California.

Because my wife's health had been poor, we decided to begin our change in life style by modifying our diet. We bought a wheat grinder and grain in bulk. We substituted bananas, raisins, and dates for white sugar and began to cook from "scratch." We began to realize that, while God has provided all the nutrition we need in the foods He created, man, aided by modern technology, has managed to drain off most of the natural nutrition and package up and sell to us what is left.

In our society, this is true for life in general. We live on a heat-and-eat, no-muss, no-fuss, uninvolved and impersonal, second-hand basis. Everything is already prepared and prepackaged for us by the manufacturer. We just "run down to the store" and buy it.

**"Prepackaged,
Pigeon-Holed,
and Polarized"**

We've been prepackaged, pigeon-holed, and polarized for the sake of convenience . . . theirs or ours?

The family unit is prepackaged and peddled in the form of the American dream: compact cars, tract houses, manicured lawns, color TV sets, and more. The mothers of our children must go to work to help support the dream, and we owe it all to credit and debt. We have substituted things for relationships in the family. *God seemed to say to us, "What shall it profit you if you gain the whole world and lose your own son?"*

**"What Shall It
Profit. . ."**

Medical care is often prepackaged. Doctors appear to know little more than to treat every ailment with some kind of drug. The personal doctor is a thing of the past. The drug business is booming. *God seemed to say to us, "Doctors, indeed, can treat, but only I can heal."*

**Only God Can
Heal**

In the schools it's prepackaged, warmed-over humanism that is doled out to children in crowded classrooms. Personal attention is at a boring minimum. Even in some Christian schools, the kids develop acid-bath vocabularies that would burn the ears of sailors. In school our children were learning to despise learning. *God seemed to say to us, "Your children are your own responsibility. Teach them yourselves."*

"Teach Them Yourselves"

Our entertainment is prepackaged. Little thinking or moving is required. The television allows us to watch life vicariously through a tube. As the world turns, you and I don't have to move a muscle. Furthermore, programs are filler for seductive commercialism.

Or just try to find an imaginative toy to stimulate your child's creativity. Places like Disneyland are showcases of the imagination of others rather than an exercise of our own. *God seemed to say to us, "All these things distract you from each other. Get rid of them."*

Getting Rid of Distractions

Worse still, salvation is prepackaged—highly processed, boxed in denominational containers, and dispensed to the local churches. There it is spoon-fed by the ministers and swallowed whole by the members, as though salvation *were* church membership, or a list of no-no's, or a commodity to acquire and put in one's pocket, rather than a living relationship with a personal Savior. *God said to us, "Abide in me."*

"Abide in Me"

I was working full-time in a Christian publishing company as an art director, product designer, graphic ad man, and illustrator. I was also an elder in our church. I wanted desperately to be a good husband and father as well as to be faithful in all of these other things, but with a house and yard to keep up on top of it all, there was little time.

I hardly knew my children, neglected my wife, took no time for friends, barely spoke to my neighbors, was frustrated with the routines of Churchianity, couldn't find a family doctor I could communicate with, knew nothing about the politicians for whom I voted, and rarely called my mother.

Though I claimed Christ as my personal Savior, I seldom spoke to Him in prayer.

What Comes First—Me, Things, People, God?

I had it all backward: me first, things second, people third, and God last.

I worked all hours to make house payments, car payments, Master Charge payments, utility bills, and insurance payments. We were crippled by an inflationary economy that forced us to buy poor quality food at outrageous prices.

Then came the Arabs with their gasoline crunch. We were caught up in a system of credit and debt that not only prevented us from enjoying each other and bound up our time, but kept us from doing what we felt God wanted to do with our lives in the first place.

What's more, the whole economic system could come crashing down on us any minute. Why not? I mean, how long can it last?

Meanwhile, Cheryl and I agreed that none of the aforementioned things meant anything to us.

What Do We Want To Do?

"I would rather paint pictures," I said.

"I would really like to spin and weave," she said . . .

We have been in northern California for months now, and no land is available yet. Inflation and the real estate investors got here before we did. We have money enough to buy only the land. We refuse to borrow from a bank to build a house. God

"God Will Supply—Board by Board, If Necessary"

will have to supply, board by board, if necessary.

If I sound like a naïve, wild-eyed romantic with notions of babbling brooks, evergreen trees, and snow-covered mountains, you're right. I am. But what else can you expect from a citified, systematized, prepackaged, out-of-touch suburbanite?

It isn't so much a nostalgic return to nature or a back-to-the-land idea that we're after, however. It is that we seek a personal encounter with God and the realities of life first-hand rather than life in a

**"He Is Our
Land, Our
Habitation,
Our King and
Defense"**

great "artificial American bubble" which is liable
to pop at any moment.

For God has made it clear to us that He is sufficient. He is our land. He is our habitation. He is
our King and Defense and our High Tower in hard
times.

A physical house would be nice, and much less
crowded than the little trailer that shelters the six of
us—Cheryl and me, a tot, a teen, and two in between! But we are willing to wait, sacrifice, live
with fewer possessions and comforts, and even
look a little foolish to follow His leading for our
family.

We teach our children at home now. The burden
of their education rests on us, where it belongs. We
have a front-row seat from which we can see for
ourselves how they are progressing academically.
No one is going to care for their education as much
as we.

We believe that the family in which the living
Christ is honored and loved as King and Lord is not
only the foundation of the local church but is the
foundry where the very characters of men and
women are forged.

**The Family As
Foundry**

Cheryl's private dream is to raise a few sheep
and Angora rabbits for wool to spin on her spinning wheel and weave into garments for the family.

My dream is to remove every encumbrance that
would prevent me from keeping my ear pressed to
His chest that I might hear every heartbeat and
desire that is His own. And that whatever I create
will be a fulfillment of His purposes and an expression of His Spirit—through art and painting and
children's books and materials that emphasize family relationships and Christian character.

Together our dream is to fulfill 1 Thessalonians
4:11-12, "Make it your ambition to lead a quiet
life, to mind your own business, and to work with
your hands just as we told you, so that your daily

Living the Home-Made, Whole Wheat, Wholesome Life

life may win the respect of outsiders and so that you will not be dependent upon anybody."

We intend to live life simply and deliberately and desire that all our "spaghetti" be home-made, whole wheat, and wholesome.

RUSS FLINT, a free-lance artist, lives "simply and deliberately" with his family in the beautiful, unspoiled wilderness of northern California. He formerly served as an officer of Dayspring, Inc.

3
THE JOY OF BEING CONTENT

In a recent issue of the *Hunger Newsletter,* published by a group of concerned Christians at Blessed Sacrament Roman Catholic Church in Rochester, New York, we read:

Today's joggers would be surprised to know that prehistoric man had no weight problems. His exercise consisted of searching, stooping, plucking the wild wheat that grew in the Nile Valley, the wild rice in Asia, the wild sorghum in Africa, or the wild corn in Mexico . . .

It was not by chance that God chose manna for His people. Wheat was the first food used in trading. Today, 53 percent of man's calories consumed are from grains—directly through bread and cereals, or indirectly through livestock, eggs, and milk . . .

Calories not only measure human energy, but measure the power of a mild wind, rushing water, and warmth of the sun. Gradually our ancestors began to use up these kinds of calories rather than his own, or to supplement his own.

This is when, and why, farming or cultivation began. He tried to decrease the use of his own calories in gaining food output. And he tried to increase the number of calories in the yield. Civilization required energy-saving and energy-cheaper ways. . .

Today's shortage of energy has little to do with the lack of enough running water, wind, or heat from the sun's rays. It has nothing to do with the lack of human energy or labor.

The beginning of the Industrial Revolution brought the beginning of the excessive use of fossil fuels. These decayed plants and animals became cheaper and cheaper to mine, or drill and refine, and to move. This form of energy was created over thousands of years ago, in the case of coal, and over millions of years for oil.

Because of our never-ending demand for more luxury, more goods, we have managed to use up these fossil fuels in two centuries! The energy crisis was produced by America and the technological West, not by the simple people of the world—many of whom have learned to be content with what they have.

Each time I return to this country after traveling abroad, the lavishness and extravagance of our Western way of life strikes me like a fresh revelation.

Other nations depend upon bicycles or motorcycles for transportation, yet when I look around the neighborhoods of my own small town, I see two and even three cars in the driveways of private homes. Indoors, furnaces and air conditioning keep the temperature constant year-round, regardless of the weather. We eat every meal as if it were Sunday dinner, with meat in abundance. Instead of preparing fresh foods, we pay high prices for canned, packaged, and frozen vegetables. Our bread comes ready-sliced and milky white, with every natural nutrient leached out of its flour. We leave food on our plates and sacrifice it to the garbage cans. On trash days I count four, five, six garbage cans or plastic bags lining each curbside. We often discard what could be repaired and used.

The Folly of Idolatry

What is even more unforgivable is the manner in which we idolatrize our money-making abilities and live as if we were the only people on earth.

The desire to decrease human labor and to increase the food supply is praiseworthy, of course. But the move toward the consumption of fossil fuels in the West, symbolized by the food industry in the above-quoted material, represents more than the desire to provide the necessities of life for those who live on this planet.

Fossil fuel-consuming societies have built military machines, conquered empires in Africa and Asia, and engaged in two world wars. As societies have grown more and more independent of human labor and more and more powerful by virtue of ever-new energy sources (steam, electricity, nuclear energy), the gap between rich and poor nations has increased proportionately.

The ability to free themselves from the limitations of human labor and the changes of the seasons have caused modern nations to worship the might and power of their own minds and the technological creations they have produced. Man, in Nietzsche's words, has made himself into a Superman. Though this image has been somewhat tarnished by recent blows to Western sources of energy, the OPEC oil price hikes, and accidents at nuclear plants, man continues to imagine himself able to accomplish anything he aspires to do. In short, He considers himself invincible—all-powerful—godlike.

> All who make idols are nothing, and the things they delight in do not profit; their witnesses neither see nor know, that they may be put to shame . . . He plants a cedar and the rain nourishes it. Then it becomes fuel for a man; he takes a part of it and warms himself, he kindles a fire and bakes bread . . . And the rest of it he makes into a god, his idol; and falls down to it and worships it; he prays to it and says, "Deliver me, for thou art my god!" They know not, nor do they discern; for he has shut their eyes, so that they cannot see, and their minds, so that they cannot understand.
>
> (Isa. 44:9-18 RSV)

Our Ultimate Concern

The joy of contentment, whether experienced only in

memories of a past life style too readily abandoned or in the midst of technological distractions, flows only from what Paul Tillich called the satisfaction of our Ultimate Concern. Contentment, so often touted as arising from an abundance of things (food, money, possessions), actually comes as a free grace from God.

Many philosophers and theologians have reminded us that wealth and ease are slippery skids that rapidly carry us away from genuine dependence upon—and faith in—God. Some theologians, like Jacques Ellul, have clearly branded technology as idolatry. Of course, this need not be so. The Hebrews knew the wheel and the bow, the axe and the inclined plane, and still knew God. Hundreds of scientists have also been priests and monks or faithful laymen.

Nevertheless, as writers from Henry Adams (*The Virgin and the Dynamo*) to Eugene O'Neill have pointed out, technology and the power it gives people, can too easily become a counterfeit god. We will not know contentment through the worship of nuclear energy or anything else that is the work of our own minds and hands.

Idolatry is always foolish, yet most of us are too blinded by self-interest to see what we are worshipping. It has always been so. This is why the prophets and the apostles and the reformers have attacked idolatry again and again throughout human history. While we may not bow down to objects made from wood or stone in our civilized culture, we often worship the more subtle and insidious idols of money, success, or sex.

A notable feature of idolatry is the manic, frenetic pace of life which it induces in the idolator. We race, we strive, we struggle to appease our god—and never quite make it. The greedy peasant who walked himself to death in Tolstoy's tale "How Much Land Does a Man Need?" was an idolator of landownership and he died in a vain attempt to satisfy an insatiable lord. The very nature of evil is that it never gives us peace but always robs us of contentment. Long ago, primitive men cried out to Moloch: "We give you our children, yet you are not content!"

Type A Believers

In recent years social scientists have written of the "Type A Personality," characterized by an obsession with work and achievement. This kind of person is particularly susceptible to heart attacks and other physical ailments caused by stress. In his book, *Coming Back,* James Johnson has written confessionally of the Type A Christian. Johnson, himself a former "workaholic," admits that while the souls of such Christians are genuinely converted, their life styles are not.

Type A believers know nothing of the rest of the soul described in the Book of Hebrews or of the mystical and satisfying union with Christ spoken of by the old-time pietists. Johnson, who denounces the "spiritual workaholic" life in his book, reminds us of a similar word from the writer to the Hebrews:

> So then, there remains a sabbath rest for the people of God; for whoever enters God's rest also ceases from his labors as God did from his.
> Let us therefore strive to enter that rest, that no one fall by the same sort of disobedience.
>
> (Heb. 4:9-11 RSV)

Further, the writer to the Hebrews makes it clear that men and women fail to enter "God's rest," to be content, because of rebellion against God.

> And to whom did he swear that they should never enter his rest, but to those who were disobedient? So we see that they were unable to enter because of unbelief.
>
> (Heb. 3:18-19 RSV)

This rebellion, this refusal to believe God's promises of provision, has led us to trust in the work of our own hands with consequent over-consumption. This is spiritual idolatry and psychological suicide. Because we cannot, will not, rest content in what God provides for us, we drive ourselves to obtain more and more, then consume it and ourselves selfishly and wastefully. Hyperactivity and gluttony are sure signs of the Type A personality.

Interestingly enough, this much-admired overachiever is held up as a model of the person who is "making it" by today's standards. He is a producer, a performer, one who "burns the candle at both ends" in order to attain his goals. And the fruits of his labors, the material possessions accumulated and the awards conferred, often grow old and stale in his pursuit to achieve still more.

Unfortunately, many religious activists, adapting this humanistic value system, also tout worldly success and possessions as the end result of "being a Christian." Celebrities are paraded across the TV screens of religious programs as models to be emulated. Once more, the implication is clear: If you strive and achieve, you've earned the right to consume and perhaps even guaranteed your seat on the front row of Heaven! Dangerous thinking—both theologically and economically. Jesus teaches balance in all things.

A Balance of Nature

Type A people are the pioneers and frontiersmen of the human race—sturdy, steady, dedicated, enduring. They are always ready for a challenge, perhaps biting off more than anyone thinks they can chew—then surprising everyone by chewing it all up and asking for more! Type A people work hard, play hard, and, when they become Christians, may fervently practice their Christianity. They may attend every function of the church, serve on committees, visit the sick and shut-ins, and vote in the business meetings—until, weary of their well doing—they fall into a state of exhaustion and depression. This is a kind of "spiritual burnout." Yet, the Type A person can't rest! There is a basic flaw within that prevents him from fully relaxing. He must always be on display, always proving himself, because *he doesn't believe in the reality of his own worth.*

Psychologists would say the Type A person is insecure, has a poor self-image, and, as a child, may have lacked the experience of acceptance by others. Biblically, the Type A Christian has not fully understood the total acceptance of the sinner by God when he confesses Christ. Type A religious activism, then, can be an evidence of a lack of faith, confidence, and trust in Almighty God. As Paul Tillich once stated in a university sermon: "The only answer to this insecurity is to *accept our acceptance.*" This acceptance must be made in the innermost feelings and emotions and not only by the intellect.

It is this insufficient faith, this failure to trust, that makes the hyperactive person run until he falls. And because it is a defect of faith, the Type A Christian turns to works to justify himself before God and other Christians.

Martin Luther, before his "tower experience" when he came to see that we are justified by faith alone without works of the law, was the classic Type A personality. He fasted, prayed, and beat his body and yet found no peace, no rest. In that state of utter futility, he actually hated God who had made His commandments so hard and Luther's flesh and will so weak. There was nothing left for him but guilt and anger—no contentment, no joy in his Christianity. With the precious insight that we are made right with God by Christ's sacrifice, which we appropriate by faith through God's grace, Luther felt as if he had entered paradise! He knew peace at last and the joy of full communion with God. Filled with that joy, he became a powerful instrument for the reformation of the church.

Finding contentment in all the experiences of life is only possible for the trusting, confident person. If we trust, belief is easy. If we lack trust, belief becomes more and more difficult. Examples of this fact aren't hard to find. If a wife trusts her husband, he may stay away all night and she will believe the explanation he gives her the next day. If she doesn't trust him, she won't believe the reason he may offer to cover a half-hour's delay by heavy traffic!

For the committed Christian who knows he is a child of God, there should be an accompanying feeling of security. We ought to be able to take an objective look at our possessions and wealth and separate our present and future security from these material protections. I have known many people who have come to this objective reappraisal of themselves only after their Type A behavior has produced ulcers or heart attacks.

In God We Trust

If we can bring ourselves to such an objective look at the things we have, we may begin to appreciate the Bible's warning not to trust in princes, arms, the strength of our own arm, or gold. We may catch a glimpse of the Provider who stands behind the provisions we have received from His hand. We may, then, experience the "rest" that the writer to the Hebrews speaks about.

That rest is not limited to one Sabbath day a week; in fact, has nothing to do with days and times and plans for our time. That rest is the continual confidence of the child of God in his Father; it is the communion of the Christian with God through Christ. The Sabbath rest is, in the theological language of the old-time pietists, "union with God." In that Sabbath rest, begun now in this life and stretching in unbroken measure throughout eternity, we find the answers to our insecurities, our fears, our doubts.

In that high communion, we can rest. We have no need to strive for further acceptance. We know, now, that we are accepted. We have not chosen Him; He has chosen us, called us, sealed us. In accepting our acceptance, we find the strength to make do in plenty or in want, and may enjoy a Sabbath rest of total joy, unaffected by the times and changes of the world.

As John Wesley said of his Aldersgate experience, "I felt my heart strangely warmed. I knew I did trust in Christ, in Christ alone, for my salvation."

When we trust in this way, we can begin to share, believing

that God will always provide—not always what we want, but what we need. Thus, we will have escaped from the idolatry of our possessions and the worship of the strength of our own arm.

LIVING THE JOY

Dean Merrill

I was a wide-eyed twelve-year-old in the fall of 1956, a season to be marked forever in automobile history as the Year of the Fin. The new models of previous autumns had come and gone with little notice, but that September, as Detroit's astounding '57s were unveiled, I discovered that Solomon must have been wrong: there was indeed a new thing under the sun.

Car Fever Strikes Early

Each afternoon as I scuffed along my paper route through the commercial area of a Missouri county seat, I could not help stopping in at a showroom or two to gaze in wonder. The Chevy's fins were straight and vertical, as if borrowed from a rocket; it was definitely a car meant to fly. The wondrous new sheet metal even made it more aerodynamically stable, said the fliers; it had been tested in wind tunnels. Ford's fins were not quite so bold, but they were placed on an outward tilt. Neither of them, however, could match the curvaceous Plymouth as it swooped up to a climax of aesthetic tingle. To a junior high boy entering puberty, it gave a rush of awe mixed with fascination.

By the next year our family had moved to Hutchinson, Kansas, and I didn't have a paper route, but I made a special pilgrimage downtown all alone the night the dealers announced an Open House for the even more spectacular '58s. I scurried from display floor to display floor, gasping and gawking. The Pontiac had a dazzling cluster of taillights that, if you sat a man's hat on top of them, became a kind of robot's face. The turn signals would then make his eyes blink while the rest of him glowed cherry red.

I was hooked. I had discovered the supreme joy of living, the key to power and enchantment, the guarantee of status and respect. A car was far, far more than a piece of transportation; it was a marvel of technical brilliance that rose above the sum of its many parts to approach personality. It was also an essential part of manhood.

I turned fourteen that winter, which qualified me in those years for a true rite of passage: a driver's license. By the next summer my foster brother and I had earned enough money to buy an aging Mercury coupe without a first gear. We eagerly tore into the transmission, bought the parts, and soon had it running. We now had a movable zone of privacy, a habitation that was ours alone, a me-place. The low rumble of its glass-packed muffler turned heads in the high school parking lot, and after we painted the car black, our self-esteem was invincible.

The Fun—and Fundamentals— Of Auto Ownership

Such an ally was not, of course, without its requirements. I began noticing a clattering sound in the engine while accelerating, and when it didn't seem to go away, I asked my father about it.

"Hey, listen to this," I said as I came to a stop sign one day. "It makes a funny noise when I take off."

He listened. A frown crossed his face.

"How long since you checked the oil in this thing?"

"I don't know."

We pulled to the side of the country road and raised the hood. The dipstick showed not a trace of black. The noise, I learned, was coming from rod bearings clattering against a flattened crankshaft, thanks to the absence of lubrication. My beloved alter ego was suddenly very sick, and it was all my fault.

We pulled the black beauty into a barn on the farm where we lived, set the front end up on blocks, and proceeded with surgery. It was an operation that took us amateurs more than a month to complete, but if you think such a trauma led me to question the passion I had embraced, you are quite mistaken. This was no passing teen-age fad. This was part of becoming an American adult. It was, in fact, a challenge, a game to master—making that engine start on subzero mornings, ramming my way through snowdrifts, skimming the asphalt stretches in the summer like a bird of prey. Fools who didn't know how to employ socket wrenches and timing lights were helpless victims in such a sport. We were its young lions.

As I left for college in Chicago, an obvious maxim of the game was that one ought to drive the newest and biggest car he (or his parents) could afford. In my sophomore year I dallied with a novelty, a long, black '48 Dodge limousine. That was soon followed by a more chic Olds hardtop, and then a pink and white Cadillac Coupe de Ville. By the time I was married, I had scrambled up to an almost-new Mercury Monterey with four-barrel carb and that classy reverse-slant window in the back.

Young Lion In a Limousine

A highlight of each year was a trip to the Chicago Auto Show, a mammoth banquet of chrome and glass and hand-polished lacquer, garnished with bright lights and full-color brochures and alluring blondes. Revolving platforms turned Detroit's finest for every possible view, and even the exotic European manufacturers made their pitch. It was, for me, a stroll through paradise.

What made automobiles so delectable, among other things, was that they were a perfectly acceptable way to parade one's financial status. You couldn't go flashing your savings account passbook, your CDs, or your stock portfolio; you couldn't announce your recent raise—but you could convey the same message through what you

**And Then—
The Awakening!**

parked out front. It was a clear indication of how you were coming up in the world.

And then came the Awakening.

It was not a flash of understanding on one day, but rather a gradual dawning of financial reality. This pursuit of automotive status, this constant push to upgrade was costing real money, wasn't it? I did some calculating and found that cars represented sixteen percent of our monthly expenditure; only housing consumed more than that. Meanwhile, my wife was feeding us on thirteen percent.

And while I knew that transportation was a basic necessity of life in modern America, did we have to do it in such elegance? I took a hard look at the "investments" I had made in my various cars. Actually, I'd never made a dime "investing" in a car; they'd all sold for less than I paid for them. Some had depreciated more slowly than others, but every one of them had gone down over the period of use, not up. Hmmm.

**Does
Stewardship
Extend to
Transportation?**

During those months, my theology began talking to me. What was stewardship all about, anyway? Stewardship was far more than a euphemism for giving in offerings; it was the whole concept of taking good care of another person's (i.e., God's) assets. If it was true that I had been granted a certain number of dollars to feed, clothe, house, transport, and otherwise care for my household as well as to support God's Kingdom, how many of those dollars could be spared for a personal ego trip?

I eventually had to admit that cars were for using, not for loving. My kicks would have to be gotten in some other way. The Monterey, which by then was showing its planned obsolescence, was replaced with a used Volvo—the first small car I'd ever owned—and driven for the next 109,000 miles. The greatest change, however, was attitudinal. The coveting stopped. Automobiles came to be viewed as perishable pieces of equipment rather than as mirrors for my psyche.

In the years since then, of course, we have all become painfully aware that transportation has a price tag. Oil in the 1970s went from less than $2 a barrel to more than $24. By the time you add up gasoline, maintenance, insurance, licenses, and depreciation for one car for a year, you've spent in the neighborhood of $2500.

What's $2500? The price of a new piano, or a three-week family vacation. Or a semester of education at a Christian college. Or two months' salary for a missionary or youth worker. Or a couple thousand New Testaments in a needy land. Or a year's food for a dozen Cambodian refugees.

Not that Christianity calls for a renunciation of cars. Automobiles are here to stay, as evidenced by the fact that one of every seven jobs in America is car-related. And in many cases, cars are the most efficient way to go. Someone has figured out that for the cost of a rapid-transit system in Los Angeles, you could buy every Los Angeles family a small car.

"What Do I Need. . . What Do I Want?"

The point is rather to draw a line between "What do I need?" and "What do I want?" If I am intent on being a good steward of God's resources, do I need more than one car? Perhaps I do, but maybe, with a little adjusting and flexing, I could manage with one.

Do I need a new car? Do I need a large car? Do I need one that's "loaded"? Kenneth Taylor, creator of The Living Bible, succumbed temporarily last year to the pressure of the times and bought a Mercedes. After two weeks of living with a miserable conscience, he bravely took it back for a refund.

"Is This Trip Necessary?"

Furthermore, we might all ask ourselves continuously: Do I need to make this trip? Does my church's calendar need to be arranged in such a way that I drive there four and five times a week?

Or might I ask the leadership to do some consolidation? Early this year the Mormons put out the word from Salt Lake City for their congregations to pull all major meetings into a single three-hour block on Sundays. The world's largest congregation, Full Gospel Central Church in Seoul, Korea, gathers only once on Sundays and ministers to its 100,000 members mostly through 6700 walking-distance cell groups all over the city. Even tithes are collected in cells.

I stopped by a showroom the other day to pick up another one of those glossy, full-color brochures. Amid exquisite photography of crushed-velour interiors and sleek body lines, the words said, "All in all, the 1980 _____ is a most attractive choice for people who feel that a full-size car is something they need—and deserve."

What do I need? A very good question indeed.

DEAN MERRILL drives a '74 Honda Civic to and from David C. Cook Publishing Company in Elgin, Illinois, where he is executive editor. He is the author of several books including The Husband Book (Zondervan). This account appeared originally in Eternity *magazine, September, 1980.*

4 THE JOY OF A GENEROUS SPIRIT

Count Leo Tolstoy, the famous Russian moralist and novelist, succinctly portrayed the view of the plain person in a short story entitled, "How Much Land Does a Man Need?"

In this tale, a group of tenant farmers are told by a nobleman that they may claim as much land for themselves as they can walk around in a day's time.

One farmer paces himself and encompasses a considerable piece of land without overtiring himself or violating the limit.

Another, however, races greedily around the countryside all day long. He dashes through valleys and puffs up hills, always seeing one more treasure—a well, a creek, a mountain—that he wishes to own. As evening approaches, the man presses on, remembering late that he must yet run back to the starting point to fulfill the requirement. Sweating and anxious, the farmer makes the deadline, only to fall dead from overexertion.

And Tolstoy voices the haunting question: "Just how much land does a man need?"

How Much Is Too Much?

For the millions of Christians living in the wealthy, developed nations of the world, this question is both disturbing and challenging. In fact the Western ethic of discipline and hard work, sometimes called "The Protestant Ethic," is often, in itself, a major reason for the accumulation of wealth.

As the author of Judges observed long ago:

> Then the Lord raised up judges, who saved them out of the power of those who plundered them. And yet they did not listen to their judges . . .
> Whenever the Lord raised up judges for them, the Lord was with the judge, and he saved them from the hand of their enemies all the days of the judge . . .
> But whenever the judge died, they turned back and behaved worse than their fathers . . .
>
> (Judg. 2:16-19 RSV)

Apparently, it is difficult for people to manage too much worldly "success" while retaining deep faith in God.

From the days of the Puritans to the present, Christianity has been associated with hard work and ensuing wealth. That longtime relationship is now changing. An assumption that prosperity is associated with virtue is challenged by those who are aware that much of that wealth has been accumulated through exploitation of others, both here and overseas. The shrinking of the world through air travel, instantaneous communications, and increased awareness of the political realities of the world have made Western Christians uneasy about their high standard of living. This uneasiness is due not only to the vast disproportion between the West and the countries of Asia, Africa, and Latin America, but to the growing awareness that our powerful, developed countries have taken from the weaker countries raw materials that they could have used themselves. For example, Brazil and other coffee-growing regions plant coffee for American use instead of crops for native use. Millions are poverty-stricken in Brazil, while a few become rich, selling us our morning "eye-opener." The only name for situations like this is exploitation. The same is true for diamonds dug by black labor in South Africa, bananas grown in Central America, and oil refined in South American nations. Our comfortable style of living is due, at least in part, to the people in "third-world" countries who have been forced to be "hewers of wood and haulers of water" for our comfort.

Of course, America and the West have also achieved power through hard work, discipline, and intelligence. We have believed the old slogan (not found in Scripture) that "God helps those who help themselves." The Protestant Ethic may be a distortion, however, of what the Gospel is all about. It seems that in helping ourselves, we have forgotten that we must refrain from taking from others. We are not commissioned by God to "help ourselves" to the possessions of other people. The truth is, we are to work hard to support ourselves and are enjoined by our faith to use our surplus for the assistance of the less fortunate. Selfishness and exploitation cannot be defended on a Scriptural basis.

Because He Gave

There are many philosophies in the world that stress giving. It's important, I think, to affirm the goodness and decency of all such outlooks.

All the great religions of the world stress charity and almsgiving. It's a moving sight to witness the poor of Moslem Africa giving alms to beggars in the "souk" or marketplace. As Christians we can affirm this kind of unselfishness and human kindness. Whatsoever things are pure and of a good report, the followers of Jesus Christ will affirm and support, no matter who performs those acts of love.

Secularized people in America and the West quite often have sensitive consciences and emphasize charity. What Christian could be opposed to such feelings and actions? In a world dominated by the original sin of pride and self-centeredness, we must greet the smallest candles of concern for other people as flames kindled by the holy fire of the living Spirit of God.

Yet Christian giving rests on something more than the residual feelings of human community that still exist here and there, despite the universal fall into sin. Christian giving grows out of more than feelings of camaraderie. It is based solidly on the decisive action of Almighty God in Jesus Christ. The distinctiveness of Christian giving derives from the fact that God gives, and because He gives to us, we feel impelled by His loving Spirit to share ourselves, His Word, and our goods with other people.

Because God gave us life, because He is our Creator, we are only stewards of His goods. What we have is not ours absolutely but is held only in trust. Because God has not been selfish with us, we cannot be selfish with others. That is the point of Jesus' parable of the unjust steward in Matthew:

> You wicked servant! I forgave you all that debt because you besought me; and should not you have had mercy on your fellow servants, as I had mercy on you?
>
> (Matt. 18:32 RSV)

But more than the gift of life itself, God has given us Himself in the Incarnation of the Savior, the God-man, Jesus Christ. We have been forgiven our sins of pride and self-centeredness and selfishness, cleansed of lust and greed. How can we, forgiven sinners, yet live as if we were still in our sin?

Forgiven sinners, which is what we all remain in this life, must constantly stress their forgiven state. There is no room for selfishness or for lust for material possessions in a life of daily repentance and faith.

Jesus Christ is the friend of sinners of all classes, places, and times. But Jesus, in His earthly ministry, found Himself most often in the company of the poor and powerless. We should be careful not to over-romanticize the poor, for poverty brings its own dehumanizing, demonic temptations. Nevertheless, we should also be aware of the openness of the humble poor in many times of history to the sheer free grace of God. A bonus of poverty *can be* (it isn't always) the communion of fellow sufferers with one another. An openness to and kinship with the great Fellow Sufferer, Jesus Christ, can be the greatest wealth of the poverty-stricken.

I have been deeply moved by the devotion of Indian peons in Mexico, who kneel devoutly before the shrines of their village churches. While much of their ritual is foreign to my Protestant eye, I can sense the openness so many of these simple people have to the Suffering Servant so graphically represented on the crucifix hanging over their old-fashioned Catholic altars. The truly devout poor feel their burdens lightened because that One on the cross shares their suffering, and they, in turn, share the burdens of one another. Underneath all the strange rituals, I have sensed the reality of the communion of the Christian with God through Christ and of the living communion of the saints.

Poverty can make or break a person. The effect of such suffering depends less on human strength and goodwill than it does upon the reality of Christian faith in the person who must bear this involuntary life style.

Giving and Sharing

There is an intriguing difference between *giving* and *sharing*. We may give simply because we have enough and more than enough for ourselves. Such giving may even be done in a spirit of genuine kindness, yet it really costs us nothing. There is no sacrifice, no giving up of something which we ourselves need.

Sharing, on the other hand, involves participation in the life of others—apportioning what we have, even out of our poverty, if necessary. To share means to divide the very means of our lives with others.

Sharing takes on new meaning when you consider that another's health or survival may depend upon your passing half of your can of beans to him. When I entered the Marine Corps at age seventeen, I was amazed that people grumbled about the food. It wasn't the best quality, but there *was* enough to go around. I was happy to have it, even when the little slabs of ice cream that were tossed on the hot mess trays melted into the pork and gravy.

Later, in the Chosan Reservoir area of North Korea, surrounded by the Chinese Army, we ran short of rations. One box of C-rations, designed for one man for one day, was distributed to *three* men for one day. Most of us were poor boys under the age of twenty and the sharing was done good-naturedly, despite the griping about the fouled-up supply.

Learning to Share

Because most of our children have not known poverty, they have grown up not knowing how to appreciate or to share what they have. Our middle-class way of life has produced some very selfish people, who have little concept of the difficulties involved in earning their daily bread or the joy that comes in sharing it with others.

Reared in plenty, our children have come to think of plenty, even luxury, as their right and may never feel gratitude to those who work hard to make that plenty available to them. I'm afraid we parents may have contributed to this "wrong end up" way of looking at the world through indulging our children. We shouldn't deny them anything good or needful, of course, but we might temper the too-materialistic lives of our youngsters with some teaching and examples on sharing.

My son, Paul, not easily impressed with prestigious labels, has learned how to be content with whatever is serviceable. Recently he remarked about the high prices of camping equipment at the Army-Navy Store. "Let's go to the Goodwill Store," he suggested. "We'll just recycle some stuff that others are finished with." Such thriftiness is a form of sharing, *even with people we have never met!* That attitude puts "things" precisely in the right place.

Barriers to Sharing

Anyone who has been exposed to the gospel of Jesus Christ realizes, at least intellectually, that sharing is the expected response to God's great gift of life and salvation. Yet not everyone who says "Lord, Lord," goes on to share, share. Why?

I believe our inability to incorporate the graciousness of Jesus into our life styles derives from a lack of full commitment to our Lord. And that lack of commitment may well stem from an inadequate appreciation of ourselves as precious persons of worth to God. In short, we may not yet believe that we have true, abiding worth simply because God is our Creator and our Re-Creator, our Renewer in the Atonement made by Jesus Christ. We may be "Christian" in our intellect but not yet fully converted in our emotions. We may still be measuring our worth in the terms of our materialistic, work-oriented culture, instead of by the standards of the Scriptures.

The standards of our culture are twofold and both contribute to self-centeredness and a grasping after possessions:

1. We measure our worth by our job performance, as indicated by our salary and other marks of "success," and

2. We measure our worth by our possessions—houses and cars and bank accounts. We turn our self-worth into things that we can touch and hold and "show off" to others.

Both of these worldly standards are completely materialistic and by-pass our spiritual centers. These standards say "I am," "I have;" not "I am redeemed," "I am loved by God."

Our own standards may be tested by asking ourselves, the question "Who am I?" If the answer, "I am a forgiven child of God," is not completely honest for us, then we may want to pray for insight into our self-image. God has the power to change our inner lives as well as our outward behavior.

The joy of the plain life, indeed any kind of real joy, is a possibility only for those who know themselves to be of supreme worth because they are forgiven children of God. We love Him because He first loved us. We do not love Him, if we truly commune with Him in Christ, because of the material blessings that may flow from a life of faithfulness.

Both the Old and the New Testaments point out the folly of loving God for what He *does* for us, rather than loving Him for who He *is*. In the Gospel of John, we read that Jesus turned in disappointment to the disciples and said:

> 'Truly, truly, I say to you, you seek me, not because you saw signs, but because you ate your fill of the loaves. Do not labor for the food which perishes, but for the food which endures to eternal life, which the Son of man will give to you; for on him has God the Father set his seal.'
> (John 6:26-27 RSV)

Moses, too, warned the Israelites in the wilderness against storing up the manna God miraculously provided. (See Exodus 16:9-36 and Numbers 11:1-35.) God did not want the Israelites to trust in the food stores they possessed but in the One who provided the food.

> Morning by morning they gathered it, each as much as he could eat; but when the sun grew hot, it melted.
> (Exod. 16:21 RSV)

Only on the eve of the Sabbath was it possible for the Israelites to gather twice as much as they needed, so they could rest on the Sabbath day (Exodus 16:22-30).

Job's often-told story also reminds us that the person of true faith does not serve God for the good things such worship often brings. When poor Job is destitute and miserable, his practical wife declares: " 'Curse God, and die' " (Job 2:9 RSV). But Job, the faithful one, answers, " 'Shall we receive good at the hand of God, and shall we not receive evil?' " (v. 10).

Job, who was a man of great wealth before God allowed Satan to test his faith, remains trusting of God's true goodness, despite his misfortunes. He rises to a vision of the coming Christ in his confession:

For I know that my Redeemer lives,
    and at last he will stand upon the earth;
and after my skin has been thus destroyed,
    then from my flesh I shall see God.

(Job 19:25-26 RSV)

We cannot serve God for bread, for the blessings of material prosperity, and claim to know Him fully. The great paradox of the Christian life is that our spiritual prosperity may lead to physical poverty. The noble army of the martyrs, who suffered the loss of every earthly possession, including life itself, is the sign and seal of that truth.

Other Sheep Not of This Fold

It is ironic that some people outside the traditional church have recognized the love of God for the poor and needy more readily than have those inside the church. Abraham Lincoln, a great and good man, but a member of no church, once observed: "God must have loved poor people for He made so many of them."

Mohandas Gandhi, called the "Mahatma" or "Great One" by millions in India, was not a Christian, but was greatly influenced by the Gospels. He declared himself to be a Hindu, but embraced the teachings of Jesus. Gandhi's life was full of activity—speaking, writing, traveling, and imprisonment—as he struggled for the independence of India. Yet Gandhi lived the simplest of lives, owning only a watch, a pair of shoes, and a few books.

It was Gandhi who began the rehabilitation of the poorest of the poor people of India, the so-called "untouchables," by renaming them "the children of God." Even though he remained a Hindu, Gandhi rejected the discrimination of the Hindu "caste" system. He saw the elegant lives of the high-caste Brahmins as contrary to everything truly religious when compared to the millions living in poverty and starving whenever drought or floods struck India. Gandhi counseled a more democratic, more loving, simpler life style for everyone.

God speaks to us in many ways, even through the lives of those not part of His visible church on earth. We can learn something from Gandhi, as well as from Socrates, the old Greek teacher who died four centuries before Christ was born.

Socrates, the Athenian stonemason and greatest of philosophers, once prayed:

> O God, make me pure in the inner man and may the inner and outer man be as one. Is there anything more, O yes, give me so much gold as a wise man can carry.

The amount of gold that a wise man can carry has never been computed, but common sense dictates that it can't be very much.

How is it possible that a civilization that has honored Socrates and Diogenes, the philosopher who lived in a tub and begged his meals, venerated Francis of Assisi, who lived in abject poverty, and worshipped Jesus of Nazareth, who had no place to lay His head, developed such a fixation on wealth?

More Precious Than Gold

Like nuclear material, gold has a way of affecting everything and everyone who comes in contact with it. One of the first signs of "gold sickness" is a restless desire for more and more possessions, fame, and power.

As the uncertainties of world political affairs and rising inflation rates continue to plague our country, the ownership of gold looms ever more desirable as a means to financial security. The U.S. law has been changed, making the ownership of gold legal for American citizens. "As good as gold" is a slogan that has taken on new dimensions.

And yet gold is not *qualitatively* different from other tangibles, like silver, platinum, paper money, stocks, and bonds. It is only one of the most desired of *extrinsic* goods—those things that are the means to the acquiring of other things. Gold in itself is good for nothing but for what it can be traded for or fashioned into. It is a means, because of human convention, to get other needed things, like food or shelter, or to be formed into dental bridgework or jewelry. Gold has no intrinsic value.

Intrinsic goods are *states of being,* intangible, non-material. Happiness is an intrinsic good; peace of mind is an intrinsic good; love is an intrinsic good, and union with God is the most desirable of intrinsic goods. These states of being are more precious than gold.

Dr. Dave Breese of Christian Destiny, Inc., writing in the April 1980 issue of *Moody Monthly,* describes several others:

Breese reminds us that *"wisdom is more valuable than gold."* "To get wisdom is better than gold" (Prov. 16:16 RSV). By wisdom the Bible means, of course, the inner prompting of the Spirit that leads us to faith in Christ.

Secondly, *"a good reputation is more valuable than gold."* "A good name is to be chosen rather than great riches, and favor is better than silver or gold" (Prov. 22:1 RSV). Those whose sinful actions have cost them their reputations know the real truth of this statement.

The Apostle Peter tells us that *"the genuineness of your faith, [is] more precious than gold"* (1 Peter 1:7 RSV). God tells us that the trials that stretch our faith to the limit are valuable beyond all possessions and good circumstances. Only the metal of faith that is tried in the fire becomes solid and firm. Adversity can be more precious than gold when we look at life from the perspective of eternity.

Finally, Breese reminds us that *an eternal soul is more precious than gold* or even of the whole of the material world. Matthew 16:26 makes clear that God's "economics" are different from those practiced by our society. We need to see the quest for souls as the only realistic approach to life, not the quest for gold. As our Lord says to the lukewarm church members in Laodicea:

I counsel you to buy from me gold refined by fire, that you may be rich . . .

(Rev. 3:18 RSV)

Sharing Christ, Sharing Oneself

The desire to amass gold and possessions is a detour on the Christian's journey to the Promised Land. Only knowing and sharing Christ is of ultimate worth. That is why the person of wisdom and faith will be attracted to the plainer life style of sharing—first of sharing Christ and then of sharing himself and his possessions.

One who knows the Lord already knows the depths of joy. There is no aching sadness within the believer that needs to be "treated" by the accumulation of "self-worth" through the acquiring of more money and possessions. *Christian sharing starts from joy—the joy of communion with Christ; it is not an activity designed to lead on to joy at some future time.* Unlike well-meaning humanistic counsels to lead simpler lives so that the person may find peace of mind and contentment, Christian sharing leads to a plainer life because *the Christian already has everything he needs!*

The person who is fully submitted to Christ freely becomes the servant of others for Jesus' sake, not out of hope for reward or for the reduction of an inner sense of guilt. The submitted, committed believer knows he needs only so much land as will support his family and provide surplus to share with others. He does not need more. The person in communion with Christ joyfully recognizes that he needs only as much of this world's "gold" as a wise man can carry—and share with the less fortunate. The wise Christian knows the foolishness of piling up money and things, for he knows he came naked into the world and will take nothing out of it, except the true treasures—faith, hope, and love—the gifts of a God in whom he will live forever.

LIVING THE JOY

Dr. Wayne G. Bragg, Phil Johnson, Debbie Davis

How can this generation of American youth, brought up in the quintessence of the materialistic "good life," learn the biblical value of joyful sharing? Our wealth makes us more grasping than giving. We know little of the experience of the Macedonian congregation who had been tried hard, "yet in all this they have been so exuberantly happy that from the depths of their poverty they have shown themselves lavishly open-handed. Going to the limit of their resources, as I can testify, and even beyond that limit, they begged us most insistently, and on their own initiative, to be allowed to share in this generous service to their fellow-Christians. And their giving surpassed our expectations; for they gave their very selves, offering them in the first instance to the Lord, but also, under God, to us" (2 Cor. 8:2-5 NEB).

To simply tell people that the Lord will judge us as to how we treat the hungry, naked, thirsty, imprisoned, and powerless is not enough. Nor is it enough to lay on them a guilt trip without offering positive alternatives for action.

One such alternative is the Human Needs and Global Resources Program of Wheaton College. Besides preparing students through classes in the theoretical issues of the problems of poverty and wealth, the program sends a number of students annually to study and serve in third-world communities. They live with local families and give of themselves in a variety of projects on nutrition, water resources, health care, agriculture, appropriate technology, cultural analyses.

They experience the joys and sorrows of daily life in a Senegalese village, an Indian community, or a squatter slum in Mexico City.

They learn much about sharing from the poor themselves who, in their poverty, still know the joy of sharing.

They return to the U.S. with a stronger commitment to living more simply and giving themselves in Christian service.

Phil Johnson wrote of this in his journal from Sialkot, Pakistan, where he has been working in health care and nutrition:

July 17-19

Today I was working in a village and my sandal broke. My host immediately took off his only pair of sandals and gave them to me. After using them, I offered them back, but he insisted they were now my sandals.

August 11

I have now worked three weeks, saving the life of Zobia, a six-month-old girl with marasmus malnutrition. When she was stronger, I took Zobia and her mother back to the village. I was told they were going to serve me a big meal. I knew they didn't have enough money and I asked them to spend the money on Zobia. They found out when I would come back to the village, however, and when I went there today, they had a feast prepared for me. I was deeply touched.

June 30

I've been in this village now for two days. My shelvar and kamis were dirty and ripped. Chamen noticed this and also the fact that these were the only clothes I had. He gave me a set of clothes and, in essence, I became his adopted son.

* * *

And from Debbie Davis, interning in Haiti, these excerpts from her spiritual dairy:

Sunday, July 6

Sunday morning and beautiful. Mornings are, in Haiti.

Sounds of American music—a lovely arrangement of "Yesterday." I should be homesick, but so far I am only enjoying the generosity and hospitality of my new Haitian Christian friends. They insist on giving me the *best* seat, the *best* dishes, the *most* food—even out of their meager supplies.

Sounds of dishes clattering, grandmère talking in French to little Claude, an occasional rooster crowing, a cow bawling, people walking and talking in the streets . . .

The prospect of church all morning and four hours of special Bible study in the country. *C'est bon!*

Yesterday, our Bible study included Dr. Philippe, her grandmother and great-grandmother (age is revered here), the three little children, Marjolie, and one of Dr. P's sisters. What a blessing to see how dedicated these women are. We are studying Philippians and they were talking (I think!) about how hard it is to live the Christian life of servanthood—moment by moment. Ah! It isn't any easier for *them*, with so many *fewer* distractions and temptations (as I see it) here than in the U.S. But Satan can attack with only *one* diversion—or even *none*, just the thought, right? The grandmother led the study and prayed a beautiful, beautiful prayer in Creole.

The Christian Life—With Few Distractions

Father, today I pray for healing for myself (my cold hangs on stubbornly) and for the sick in Haiti—*a big request*. Most of all I pray for Your wisdom. How do I act? What do I say? (Thank You for forced silence—I don't know the words anyway.) Show me when to speak or move. Guide me and keep Satan far away. The voodoo drums are loud, but the silence of Your Presence is louder still. *Merci, Bon Dieu!*

Friday, July 18

Yesterday I had to cry. A man and woman brought their little son to the clinic. He was eighteen months old, they said, but looked more like eight months and was almost dead from third-degree malnutrition. His little brain must be damaged—he'll never be what You intended, Lord!

Who Is To Blame?

I'm at a loss. Did You plan it that way? Where does Your sovereignty, those parents, and our responsibility meet? I wanted to blame the parents—but they haven't been taught. I could blame those in the educated world who don't teach what they know. I suppose it boils down to the fact that man's sin has created a world where there can be a Haiti.

One thing I know—You are teaching me patience here and how to make room in my heart for people who are different from me. Mold me—break me, if You have to—stretch me even if it hurts, because I want to be known as *Your* vessel here—not as the American named "Debbie."

Mold Me, Break Me, Stretch Me

Wednesday, August 6

It's been only a week since I arrived in Haiti. Lord, how much You have taught me! How much I have yet to learn!

And now, You have taken us safely through a hurricane here in Turbe. I never felt fear because we are fortunate enough to be housed in a strong building, and You are here. If I had spent the night in a mud hut, would I have been afraid?

Lord, how I prayed for You to protect these people. So far, we haven't heard of any deaths. Thank You! Yet, Father, the cleanup will begin soon, and people will be hungry because food will be scarce—and charbon for cooking fires, all wet. Lord, send some relief. Give us our daily bread. (For the first time in my life, I find myself praying for *food*, yet it constantly amazes me that the people here share whatever they have with anyone in need!) Let my family and friends at home have peace about my safety. And send that hurricane out to sea!

Monday, September 1

Today I got seven letters! Hallelujah! It's thrilling to hear from home that my church family and relatives had been holding me up in their prayers throughout the hurricane. Communication is so slow here. For two weeks, they didn't know if I was still here or had been blown away! Yet each of them mentioned the peace that had come only from You, Lord! You are so faithful!

And a letter from a friend working in Uganda reminds me that I am not the only one experiencing the joys of Your provision. Evelyn Farris writes: "Mom, dad, and I visited a woman one day and took her some clothing and other things. You would not have believed the house she lives in with her three daughters—only six feet by twelve feet with mud walls and floor. To enter, we had to crawl through a tiny opening. Inside, it was so dark that we could barely make out a mat on the floor where the four of them sleep, with their few possessions on top. To the side of that was a kind of fireplace where all the cooking is done. The little place was thick with smoke. I shuddered to think that people really do live like this.

"You can imagine our joy in being able to provide this family with some bedding and clothing. But the deeper joy came to us several weeks later. We had shared in our Bible studies with the woman's sons the blessings and responsibilities of Christian giving and had read and meditated on Ephesians 4:28: "Let him that stole steal no more; but rather let him labour, working with his hands the thing which is good, that he may have to give to him that needeth." (These people are so poor that stealing is a real problem.)

"One day when one of the boys was visiting his mother, a widow who lives nearby stopped in. She was dressed, as most of the peasants here, in rags. Moved by the Spirit, the boy and his mother gave to this widow one of the dresses we had given to the mother. Then they encouraged her to thank Jesus rather than them! Just think on this! Giving out of their poverty and giving in the Spirit.

"Sometimes I feel as if my heart is going to

burst, I am so happy! Jesus is so very real, so very alive, so very personal! Praise and glory and honor to the Precious Lamb who was slain that we might be set free from ourselves and from our sin, to know Him, love Him, honor Him forever!''

DR. WAYNE G. BRAGG is associate professor of Social Sciences and directs the Human Needs and Global Resources (HNGR) program at Wheaton College, Wheaton, Illinois. His students, PHIL JOHNSON and DEBBIE DAVIS, are natives of Pakistan and Nashville, Tennessee, respectively. Portions of this account appeared originally in the March 1981 Newsletter of the Ugandan Mission Committee.

5 THE JOY OF BEING NEIGHBOR

In the neatly manicured, provincial patchwork of suburbia, in elegant glass-and-steel high-rise apartment buildings, in the crumbling, fetid squalor of the inner city, in geriatric "ghettos" disguised as nursing and convalescent homes—we have lost our sense of "neighborhood." There are plenty of people everywhere—but very few who care for one another. We have forgotten how to be neighborly. Not only do folks no longer chat over the back fence, but the back fence itself is missing!

It is not too late, however, to begin a program of reconstruction. Committed Christians, seeking to live out the new obedience, can initiate a rebirth of neighborliness—rebuilding, slowly and carefully, a network of neighborhood associations and friendships. We need not all flee to the country or the mountains to enjoy a plainer life. If the essence of the "plain person" lies in one's attitudes and conformity to the example of Jesus, the Plain Man, then we must learn interdependence and mutual trust and aid wherever we are. Nor is it necessary to establish a commune or occupy the same space in order to foster a community where we can live in real touch with one another.

Homes Where Love Is

There are, of course, those who are already building such supportive, Christlike neighborhoods. Even in our suburban area, settled only over the past dozen years, there are strong neighborhood ties, despite the frequent transfers that affect faculty and executive families. (One house nearby has been occupied by four different families in the eight years since we built our own home.)

Our nearest neighbors, separated from us by a field, have been steadfast sources of help and comfort through the years. Our daughters have served as babysitters for their three children; and our son, Paul, is now Den Chief for the Scout troop that meets in their home—and includes their two sons. Pete has helped me with car and lawnmower repairs more times than I can count. And we watch out for each other's homes whenever one of us is out of town, taking in the mail and newspapers and checking on the sump pump and the heat.

It is sometimes adversity that brings us together as real neighbors and not just people who live on the same block. The Blizzard of '78 closed roads in our small Midwestern town, interrupting electrical service and bringing community life to a halt. Since we had no fireplace, we were left without heat on the first day of the storm. To keep warm, all five of us piled into bed and bundled up under all the blankets we could find!

When the one utility that had not failed us—the telephone—rang, it was Pete, inviting us to share their home for the duration of the storm or until the power was restored. Feeling that we would soon have electricity again, we declined. But as the hours passed and the massive storm continued to rage, we grew colder and hungrier.

When the telephone rang again, the caller was a Methodist minister who lived nearby. Because of our busy schedules, Ron and I had not had many opportunities to know each other well.

When he mentioned a roaring fire and hot soup bubbling in the pot, we decided it was time that our families became acquainted!

Trudging through the blinding snowstorm to Ron's house was the beginning of a grand adventure. We were greeted by a warm fire and a warmer welcome. For five full days we remained snowbound, enjoying the hospitality of our "new" neighbors. With no television to entertain them, the children relearned the simple pleasures of books and games. What could have been a disastrous experience proved to be a unique introduction to the fine art of "neighboring."

The Hearth Revisited

The Great Blizzard of '78 taught us another valuable lesson. We must adapt our house to protect us from future energy failure.

Ironically, the most advanced technological societies are most susceptible to dysfunction. In the nineteenth century, before the widespread use of electricity, inclement weather was of little consequence. Woodburning stoves and oil lamps provided plenty of heat and light. Our experience with the blizzard convinced me that we needed to prepare for the future by looking to the past. We would begin by constructing a fireplace and chimney.

In real "plain person" style, I looked around for used bricks for this project. I discovered that someone had torn down an old barn and bulldozed the brick foundations into a pile. This "discovery" came through the kindness of a friend, who told me about the bricks. The owners graciously granted permission to haul away as many as I needed. Using my ancient station wagon, I hauled hundreds of those bricks home, working at night after work, even in the cold and rain. On weekends I cleaned them with hammer and chisel, chipping away the bits of mortar. After several sessions I had a handsome pile of used bricks, along with a dandy set of blisters on my hands! Weeks later we could look with real pride and satisfaction at the newly completed chimney, brick heat shield against the inside wall, brick hearth, and Franklin stove (which I purchased and installed).

For fuel I scavenged the ends of boards and debris from construction sites in the area, dead trees from my neighbors' yards, and trees that had been felled by a pipeline construction crew. On another occasion I helped some friends clear a wooded area on a farm and brought some of the wood home. Those old trees are now cut and stacked neatly against my garage. In this manner my neighbors and I are helping to clean up the environment while saving both energy and money.

Our own pleasure is enhanced on cold winter nights when we can open our doors to friends and neighbors—and strangers seeking the warmth of our hearth.

A Compelling Question

The familiar parable of the Good Samaritan found in Luke's Gospel (10:29-37) was used by Jesus to answer the Pharisee's question, "Who is my neighbor?" Most of us can recite by rote the facts of that story. A man on his way to Jericho was attacked and robbed by thieves and left for dead. Though several "religious" sorts passed by and saw his plight, they quickly moved on to other duties without offering him any assistance. The one who showed kindness to the poor fellow, a despised Samaritan, was truly a neighbor—or, as modern translations have it—a "fellow man."

All of us know the story and most of us believe its message, yet how many of us fully obey Jesus' command: "Go, do the same"? In an age of materialism and inflation, of threats to the maintenance of our comfortable life styles or our reputations, few of us want to put into practice the logic of Jesus' teaching: "Whoever needs me is my neighbor."

We speak of love over and over in our churches and seek to exorcise, by our words, the clear meaning of Jesus' call: Love means being a neighbor, a helper to people in need. Nor do we bother to take seriously the words of James, the brother of our Lord, when he said: "What does it profit, my brethren, if a man says he has faith but has not works? Can his faith serve him? If a brother or sister is ill-clad and in lack of daily food, and one of you says to them, 'Go in peace, be warmed and filled,' without giving them the things needed for the body, what does it profit? So faith by itself, if it has no works, is dead'' (James 2:14-17 RSV).

How do we respond when confronted by human need? How many pictures of starving children in Asia and Africa must we see before we are moved deeply enough to help? How many families in our own communities suffer lack while we choose to remain uninformed and uninvolved? How selfish can we be and still profess to be genuinely Christian?

A modern novelist has written of a disturbing paradox noted between his childhood spent in poverty, and his adult years now spent in plenty. When the writer was a boy living in a cold-water flat, no child who was visiting at suppertime was ever sent home. The little that was served was shared with all who were present. Now, he observes, other children visiting his $200,000 home are sent home at mealtime. And he ponders, *How did we have so much then when we were poor—and so little, now that we are wealthy?*

The Plenty of Poverty

That question haunts me as I sit in my comfortable home, in the fifth decade of my life. Yet there are traces of happiness, even real joy, in the memories of my own past.

I remember the poverty—and human warmth—of life in the rural South, at the end of the Depression. In my mind's eye, I can see myself awaken in the unheated, bare board bedroom I shared with my brother.

We rose early in the mornings, when the bright Southern sun broke through the torn green window shades, falling in dust-packed beams upon the scruffy blankets that dressed our beds. Two iron bedsteads jammed close together almost filled the tiny, unfinished room, leaving only a short path to the doorless entry to the kitchen where the woodstove was already sending scorched smells of grits and yesterday's heated wash water throughout the three-room shack.

Pulling on our trousers and slipping into our hightop shoes (for we slept in shirts and sweaters), we walked vigorously through the kitchen, where mother was frying mush for breakfast, and pushed open the handmade back door to run for the outhouse, thirty-five yards away. "Hurry right back to the table, children!"

Flies buzzed busily in the gray board two-holer. A torn Sears, Roebuck catalog lay on the floor and a bitter mist steamed up through the open seats from the warmer matter below.

Racing to the back porch, we washed in cold water that we poured into a chipped basin, which rested on the rickety shelf that formed one side of the porch. Drying on a damp and much-stained towel, we entered the now-hot kitchen to sit at a blue linoleum-covered table, where father was sipping his coffee and talking with mother.

There was no milk, for we usually had no cow. But there was hot mush, with occasional bits of fatback bacon, and lively conversation—and a great deal of love. Though there were few material possessions in that home, we were rich.

People visited then, too, and helped one another. No matter how frequent the visitor, he was always greeted warmly and invited to come inside or to sit on the porch. There was always a steady stream of people—bringing warmth and vitality to our bleak existence.

The local preachers came to our house, carrying black-bound Bibles, stamped in gold. (I can remember the first time I saw a red-letter edition of the New Testament. Not jaded by new things everyday, as we are now, I thought it marvelous.) There were neighbors, bringing steaming containers of homemade soup when there was illness or an extra "hand" when rain threatened our scanty harvest. And on several grand occasions, the school principal came to call, generally for the evening meal. I can still see the white-haired, white-mustachioed old gentleman who presided over our consolidated school. He loved soup, straining it through his quickly discolored mustache.

Everyday, anywhere people gathered—at the A & P Grocery, at the bank, at church (even when there were no services)—there always seemed time to visit. Even the funeral parlor was a popular spot to stop for a chat with the long-bearded patriarch who oversaw the last solemn rites due the departed. As a young schoolboy, I stopped in often to talk with this venerable member of our church, whom I, and several generations before me, called "Uncle" with great reverence and affection. The twinkle in his eye belied his sober profession, and he always looked to me like a pink-cheeked Santa Claus.

People talked to the rural mail carrier, hanging on to the side of his boxlike automobile, gaining more information orally than they read in the letters he brought or even in the weekly county newspaper.

There are still places where people live like that. Blessed are they. We need to recover that tribal, family-like atmosphere once again. Something precious has been lost in our great strides toward wealth and upward mobility. I strongly suspect that, most of all, we have lost the simple joys of daily living and social intercourse. We must recover that joy, if we are to live life humanely, in sound emotional and mental health.

The Cost of Keeping Up

Those memories of a simpler past in which human values outweighed money or possessions seem now to have been displaced by a destructive competitive drive.

There is a less than subtle pressure to conform to or even to excel the living standards imposed by those living around us. The neighborhood "image" is reflected in the number and model of the cars parked in the driveways, the clubs and organizations to which family members belong, even the style of dress worn. The youngsters today who dress in faded jeans have nothing on me!

Jesus warned that the "rich man" was foolish to trust in his worldly goods, for all the money in the world could not save his life when his appointed hour came (Luke 12:13-20). "So is he who lays up treasure for himself, and is not rich toward God" (Luke 12:21 RSV).

Ancient Greek legend tells us of an historical figure whose life and death perfectly illustrate the truth of Jesus' parable of the rich fool. Croesus, king of Lydia, was one of the richest men in the ancient world. Not content with his vast resources, he decided to plunder the neighboring country of Persia. To discover what might happen if he carried out his plan, Croesus sent a messenger to consult the famous Oracle at Delphi. The Oracle, speaking in vague and mystical terms, said: "If Croesus attacks Persia, a great empire will fall."

Blinded by greed, Croesus interpreted the message to mean that he would conquer Persia. But the defeat was to be his own! Angered by his aggression, the Persians countered the attack and captured Croesus and all his possessions. The conquerers piled high his treasures, bound him, threw him on top, and set fire to the great heap. As the flames swept toward his body, Croesus spotted one of the seven wise men of Greece standing by. He berated the sage, claiming that the Delphic oracle had misled him. "Not so," the dying king was told. "The Oracle's prediction has come to pass. A great empire has fallen—the empire of Croesus. Croesus has been misled by greed alone."

Greed. We are all guilty.

The Tyranny of Things

Possessions can literally kill. Too many things crammed into a building can turn it into a firetrap. Every year we read of recluses who are found dead in homes filled with boxes of unopened goods. Occasionally, we hear of other such disturbed people who have starved to death, though they may have thousands of dollars stashed away under their mattresses. The possession of money and things doesn't guarantee health and welfare.

Even when we do not crowd our houses with junk, the number and variety of mechanical and electrical devices contained in an average dwelling can turn life with them into a burden. Caring for things can take up more time, it seems, than the labor they are designed to save! Think of the worry, money, and time we spend in keeping one or more cars in good repair. Consider the effort to keep the furnace, the air conditioner, the refrigerator, the washer, dryer, dishwasher, garbage disposal, humidifier, dehumidifier, vacuum cleaner, radio, television, iron, telephone, typewriter, tape recorder, stereo, mixer, toaster, frypan, lawnmower, piano, electric blanket, electric toothbrush, hairdryer, electric knife, electric can opener, curling iron, and electric shaver in repair! Sometimes, after hauling several broken devices to the shop and paying out large sums for repair work, I wonder just who is the master and who is the slave. Such "labor-saving" machines are not cheap, nor is the electricity or the gasoline used to power them.

Some, like the young artist who wrote of his experiences in an earlier chapter, have left such encumbrances behind and set out in search of closer communion with God and other fellow creatures.

Finding Community

Such a dramatic renunciation of possessions may not be required of all Christians. Yet we may envy this young family who will soon experience the joys of real community. Neighbors from adjoining farms will rally to help with the felling of trees and the raising of a house, built with lumber from the land. There will be friendly conversation over meals prepared from foods grown abundantly in that fertile area. The children will grow strong and pink-cheeked in the clean, unpolluted air. And at night, weary from honest labor, their sleep will be deep and untroubled. Through the years, as the family lives in communion with the Father and community with others, they will learn absolute dependence upon God and neighbor.

I wonder, too, if sometimes the wealthier classes do not envy the poor—not so much for what they do not have, but for what they *do* have—an intact system of interpersonal relations that provides support in good times and in bad. The poorer ethnic groups in the United States—the blacks, Hispanic Americans, and Eastern Europeans—are to be envied, at least in one respect. When we view the crowded streets of their neighborhoods, we see more than garbage and junked cars. We feel a lively, throbbing, pulsating life force. People sitting on the steps in the summer night, talking to each other. Children playing stickball in the streets. Neighbor calling out to neighbor in hearty greeting. Despite all the other dehumanizing circumstances of their existence, they are together. They belong to a community, to "La Raza," the family of all those who share a skin color or a language. This richness of life is often lacking in the streets of white suburbia.

There is an element of isolation in the single-family dwellings of our residential communities. Thinking we have no real need for our neighbors leads, not to security, but to loneliness. True wealth lies in fellowship. Joy grows out of communion and community. We must learn to love one another or, finally, die spiritually, walking through the world without compassion, generosity, or trust.

Building Neighborhood Networks

An old saying has it that "If you want a neighbor, you must be a neighbor." Sometimes, I feel, we expect more from others than we are willing to do for them. "Being neighbor" means action, sharing, thoughtfulness, and awareness on a steady, reliable basis. One way in which we might build more supportive, Christ-like neighborhoods would be by building a network of support and mutual aid with those who live around us.

Many communities already have instituted "block watch" or similar programs designed to guard against crime. In such programs, neighbors agree to "watch" the houses of owners who are away from home for extended periods or during working hours. Other programs exist to guard school children as they walk to and from school. When needs of individual neighborhoods are determined, measures can be taken which will guarantee the safety and welfare of all.

Beyond these "big issue" networks to prevent crime and protect children, we might consider sharing ownership of expensive equipment, such as riding mowers, mulchers, and power saws. Why should *every* home have a whole arsenal of expensive, energy-consuming equipment? For centuries neighbors have "loaned" tools to each other.

Sharing labor with neighbors is another aspect of the "neighborhood network" system which could be mutually profitable. Why should we exchange money when I can cut your grass if you will babysit my children?

Neighborhood networks can free us from the need for large amounts of money and actually give us more time to enjoy with our families.

Trusting in a Non-Trusting World

However, building a real neighborhood is difficult today, not only because of the fast pace of our lives and the emphasis upon the nuclear family living in one-family dwellings. Along with the individualism of our life style goes an increasing sense of fear and distrust brought about by the rise of breakins, muggings, and rape—the kinds of violent crimes that so disfigure our society. In many places we live fearfully behind doors with two or more deadbolt locks and with peepholes to identify visitors before admitting them to our homes. In high-rise apartments and in the inner cities, the distrust level is understandably higher.

How can we build neighborhood networks in the face of this distrust? The answer to that is not easy, but it is simple for the Christian. We must earn the trust of others by being consistently caring and trustworthy. We begin this process by being friendly whenever we have opportunity, by being patient and agreeable, by seeking out needs in our community and attempting to fill them. Winning the trust of people who have been conditioned to distrust is a time-consuming process. But it is imperative. Only as we are willing to be salt and light, perhaps even at risk to ourselves, can we hope to preserve the meaning of brotherly love.

A Modern-Day Samaritan

This truth was made strikingly obvious to me in an experience during my seminary days. I was sent out to supply the pulpit at a rural church in upcountry South Carolina. On the way, my old car had a flat tire. Dressed in my black preaching suit, I got out and stared at the damaged tire, wondering how I could possibly change it without getting dirty. Just then an elderly black man, obviously very poor, came along. He took one look at the situation and offered to change the tire. Though I protested, he insisted and set about to make the repairs. After tightening the last bolt, he stood to his feet, wiping his hands on his already stained and dirty overalls. I offered to pay him for his services, but he refused to accept anything. "If a man can't help somebody else in need, he ain't much of a man," the old gentleman observed.

His deed, as well as his wise observation, has remained in my memory for nearly twenty-five years. This man's actions illustrate for me the meaning of the Parable of the Good Samaritan. Love, neighborliness, and kindness are basically *actions*, not *feelings* or *words*.

"Which . . . of these . . . proved neighbor to the man who fell among robbers?" asked Jesus. (Luke 10:36 RSV) And the answer comes to me in the memory of that kind deed performed so many years ago. We are Christians, neighbors, when we prove what we are by our actions. Loving costs something: giving, hard work, taking risks, even suffering. "Not every one who says to me, 'Lord, Lord,' shall enter the kingdom of heaven, but he who does the will of my Father" (Matt. 7:21, RSV).

The true joy of seeking and finding a simpler, plainer life is that we are thereby enabled to break through our selfishness and become—indeed—a neighbor to our fellow human beings.

LIVING THE JOY

Monroe and Joe Ann Ballard

On a modest, sun-drenched street in Memphis, just blocks from the squalor of the ghetto, live Joe Ann and Monroe Ballard—a most extraordinary young couple. Through the door of their small home, expanded now by ten do-it-yourself rooms, have passed some 250 youngsters—most of whom came to dinner and stayed to find a quality of life that money can't buy.

Memphis, Tennessee, typical of many large cities, has more than a thousand agencies, services, clubs, and organizations that specialize in helping people. The list goes on and on.

In fact, it has become so long that many of these agencies are providing duplicate services. But most of them have little idea what the others provide. A person seeking help is frequently in the dark about where to turn. Many are bounced from one place to another in the game of "agency referral."

The Game of "Agency Referral"

To Joe Ann, who has worked in several social service agencies, the game is familiar. "Many of them play 'pass the buck' very well. With so many services available, it's easy to send people who need help to another address."

The Ballards remember one woman whose Social Security benefits were mysteriously cut off. After trying to explain the problem to the local Social Security office, she called the Ballards in frustration. Joe Ann dialed the office to see what she could find out.

"I'm sorry, ma'am, but we can't release that information to you," said a bored voice at the other end of the line.

"But I sent you a notarized letter from Mrs.

Smith authorizing me to handle her business. It should be in the files," Joe Ann explained.

"The files are in another department. There's nothing we can do."

"May I talk to your supervisor?"

"He can't be reached at this number. He's on another line."

"May I have that number?"

"Sorry. I've been instructed not to release that information."

So the conversation went. When Joe Ann realized she wasn't getting anywhere, she hung up and called again—and again—and again. Finally, when it became clear that she wouldn't give up, she was transferred to a supervisor. After an apology, he settled the problem.

Stretching the Budget To Help Others

At Christmas one year a woman with a serious skin disease called the Ballards from her hospital bed. She had been trying to find someone who could help her buy Christmas presents for her eight children. Already she had talked to nine agencies. Since it was late in the season, none of them could provide clothes, food, or gifts for all the children. "We just don't have enough money in our budget right now," she was told.

The Ballards didn't have enough money in their budget, either, but they called several department stores and food markets. Within four hours, they had rounded up Christmas presents for the children and food supplies.

One request for aid came from the office of a government official in Washington, D.C. A staff assistant called to ask whether the couple could provide food and diapers for the family of a man who had been accidentally shot. Joe Ann and Monroe put together a basket of food, bought the diapers, and headed for the house of this family whom they had never met. They were happy to help. But they were also disappointed that neither the official nor the aides in his office thought of offering the help themselves.

"It does seem strange, doesn't it?" Joe Ann puzzled, shaking her head. "They call us—two people with no resources other than our own—to take care of this need. Our two salaries are nowhere near what that man earns. I doubt if they would equal his expense money."

The Ballards realize that an elected government official has a constituency of thousands of poor people. He couldn't help them all with money from his own pocket. But they also believe that people, whatever their jobs, should recognize their individual responsibility to care for others. It isn't a new idea, of course, just one that has been lost somewhere along the way.

People Helping People

Joe Ann and Monroe have tried to transfer the tradition of neighborliness to Memphis. They don't oppose social service agencies. They often work with them to help people. But they realize that programmed aid has its limitations. They feel strongly that the most worthy organizations can't take the place of people helping other people.

They base that belief on the success of their own work—their ability to do what institutions often cannot do. They become friends with the people whom they help. This means they can respond to individual needs. Because they work with people in their home, they can show them how to lead more useful, efficient lives. *Showing* is better than *telling*. They hire no employees, so they avoid the hassle of supervision and employee dishonesty. With no red tape or restrictive regulations, they don't require "clients" to spend hours filling out forms. Since they feel they're "on call" as Christians at all times, they don't stop answering their phone nor do they lock their door at 5 P.M.

Showing Is Better Than Telling

"An institution has to spend much of its time protecting itself," Monroe points out. "It has to worry about getting the next grant, making sure that no one is cheating, and developing good relationships with the people and organizations who support it. We don't have to protect ourselves like that because our organization is simple. We're the headquarters *and* the field representatives.''

Unfortunately, the Ballards' work has one obvious limitation. Since their organization is simple and person-centered, they can help only a few people at one time. They can't minister to the masses. In a wishful tone, tinged with hope, they speak of an ideal world where every person recognizes his duty to others. This is the responsibility of all faiths, they believe, but it especially applies to Christians.

We Are Our Brothers' Keepers

''The Bible instructs us to serve as our brother's keeper,'' Joe Ann says. ''We're supposed to care for the poor, the widows, and the orphans. But in our denomination, at least in the black churches, there's probably no more than half a dozen people who are concerned about the physical needs as well as the spiritual needs of people. Many Christians think that if they just pray for a person, God will take care of his physical needs. But the Bible makes it plain that we should get involved in meeting those needs ourselves.''

Unfortunately, Monroe points out, many Christians seem to be neglecting their responsibility in this area. Joe Ann is quick to agree. ''Too many Christians leave it to somebody else, who passes it on to another person. It's almost like an agency referral.''

The Ballards have heard every selfish excuse in the book that people use to avoid becoming involved in a ministry to the poor.

But perhaps the biggest hindrance to helping is the feeling of many people that they can't really change things. Many are bogged down in the fatalistic belief that their efforts really wouldn't do any good.

The Power of Selfishness

The Ballards would like to change the trend, stamp out selfishness, and convince others that they *can* make a difference. They have no political power and don't want it. They don't believe in marches or demonstrations. They don't have advanced degrees in political science or sociology. They are simply one couple—a sixth-grade teacher and a social worker—who have taken their Christian commitment seriously. They have found that giving is rewarding and that, even in a country of 200 million, it is possible to have an impact.

"We have to revive the individual's belief in his own responsibility," Joe Ann emphasizes. "We need people who are totally committed to the task of helping others. This is what it will take to wipe out poverty. We know it won't happen today or tomorrow. We may have to die before our philosophy is fully accepted. But we believe it can be done."

MONROE BALLARD is an elementary school teacher in the Memphis Public School system. His wife, JOE ANN, directs the Neighborhood Christian Center, an affiliate of Young Life, in addition to caring for her large and growing "family." Among other honors, this outstanding couple has received a Congressional citation for community service.

THE JOY OF PLAIN WORSHIP

6

The country church sat at the south corner of a dirt crossroads, some twenty miles from the county seat. Viewed from the wooden bench at the country store across the road, it resembled a white shoe box with rough-cut side windows and wooden front door. That church seemed not much bigger or better-built than the playhouses my brother, sister, and I often made from old shoe boxes and placed in the dirt of our front yard, landscaping the area around them with small pine cones.

The church was unadorned with sign or decoration of any kind. It just *was*. Yet, after dark on Sunday and Wednesday nights, that crude building took on supernatural dimensions. The joyful and mystical events that occurred there, often spilling out the open door and windows into the surrounding area, created an aura of innocence and reverence.

That was a Pentecostal church, I suppose. I was far too young to take notice of such details as denominational labels. We normally attended church several miles away, but my father occasionally took us children to the evening services held at the little white church. After the formality of our own services, the sequence of events there amazed me. The people sang and danced and cried. Healings were performed. People confessed their sins publicly. The aura about the place both disturbed and fascinated me.

As with so many other things my father did, I later recognized his great wisdom in exposing his children to many and varied experiences, from church to court trials to visits to the chain gang camps that dotted that section of the South. From the various religious services, I gained the insight that there is a joy in simple worship. Indeed, it often seems the more simple the setting, the more joyful the event. Complexity need not mean profundity. God speaks in many and various ways, today as always.

Worship in Many Lands

One of the more salutary things an American Christian can experience is a visit to a non-Western country and involvement in a Christian church in that very different setting. During the course of a lifetime of travel, I have had this opportunity many times. Because of the nature of this travel—military service and scholarly research—my experiences vary from those of missionaries. But the contrast with our North American middle-class life style is still pointed up.

When my son, Paul, and I were traveling through Morocco in the summer of 1980, we were impressed by the culture and the severe beauty of the land. The Moroccans were helpful and friendly and we enjoyed our visit, with one exception—the sight of the sick and the maimed. Many seemed to be afflicted by some form of crippling injury or disease which, in all probability, would have been correctable by surgery in advanced nations. We looked at these people limping along and realized that their ailments, perhaps endured since childhood, had never been treated at all.

Paul and I didn't remain in the coastal cities, but traveled by bus and train deep into the interior. I recall the stark face of poverty where the people lived on the edge of survival. Much of it could be seen from the train, as it rumbled through the dry countryside. The tents and thatched-roof adobe huts of the open plains were replaced by shanties and shacks made of old boards and rusty tin, clustered dejectedly near the limits of cities and towns. People lived out their lives in such three- or four-foot-high piles of refuse, with their children and their animals and the round, hard Berber bread that is the staple of their food. Yet, everywhere, signs advertised Coca-Cola and Western products. And both adults and children clamored for American T-shirts, asking every traveler for something from America—that ideal to which they all seem to aspire. Nevertheless, the devotion of the faithful could be seen at both Christian churches and Moslem mosques.

Celebration of Simplicity

In growing up, I experienced the church as most of us know it—in middle-class, well-dressed congregations. My occasional visits to small, rural, poor black churches or white Pentecostal meetings were so different from the mainline churches I attended in town that I gained impressions and insights I could not fully understand at the time.

At the age of seventeen, I took part in the Marine landing at Inchon, South Korea. When dawn broke that first morning ashore, I looked up from the gravel beach to see a small church, looking very much like one from home. I was amazed at the realization that there were Christians in such a strange place. Unfortunately, that church, like most buildings in that area, was heavily damaged by shell fire.

Some time later, after being wounded, I was moved to a hospital in Japan. When I was able to get around in a wheelchair, the fine Christian surgeon who had operated on me took me into the city of Yokusuka to attend church. The small congregation met in a basement. There was little in the way of furnishings that resembled a church, and I couldn't understand all that was going on. These people not only spoke Japanese (which I understood quite poorly), but also spoke in tongues! Yet, there was a tremendous spirit of Christianity in that crowded basement. For the first time in a year, I felt surrounded by loving, accepting people.

The songs were from another world, although occasionally a tune sounded familiar. I sat through it all in awe-struck silence and was sorry when that unintelligible service was over. When the doctor started to move my chair to the exit, calling for assistance to carry me out to his car, I discovered I didn't want to go.

Christianity—and Christian communion—is the same everywhere, no matter how unusual or simple the setting.

Years later, I hitchhiked around the island of Puerto Rico, sleeping on the floor of a pastor's house, attending church in little cinderblock buildings, and touching the pulse of a vigorous Christian life, even in the slums of San Juan. Since then I have seen the poor, dilapidated churches attended by believers in Greece, the wooden chapels in quiet forests in Finland, and mission stations in Africa. On vacations to Western Canada, I've felt honored to preach in small frame German Lutheran churches, set out on the rolling plains.

Christianity still is very plain in many parts of the world. Even where it is practiced in beautiful churches with elaborate rituals, it is in essence a call to a modest life style. The Founder of our faith was humble and His exaltation to glory is by God, not man.

The essential simplicity of Christianity communicated itself to me even in services I attended at St. Peter's Basilica in Rome. Even in that lavishly decorated church, the essence of devotion to God and love for our brothers and sisters was evident. I have had the same experience in St. Stephen's Cathedral in Vienna; in the great, white Lutheran cathedral in Helsinki; in the Cathedral of St. John the Divine in New York City; and in Christopher Columbus' Cathedral in Barcelona, Spain.

Truly, the greatest leader of the modern Roman Catholic Church was the good Pope John XXIII, that loving and simple man who simplified religious ritual and stressed Christian love for all human beings. The mark of John's emphasis upon simplification is everywhere to be seen—even at the site of his grave.

Pope John's burial place in St. Peter's, marked by art depicting Christ helping the poor, is a testimony to his simplicity. His monument is modest and hard to find amid the old-fashioned pomp and ornateness of the great cathedral.

This essential simplicity, under the cover of ornate forms, was brought home to me once in Philadelphia. I visited an Eastern Orthodox Church and was invited to participate in the Liturgy of St. James. The service lasted for hours, but it was essentially a repeated plea to worship God through Christ, and to learn to love one another better. The church itself stood in a poor section of the city. Its mission was to the humble, not the proud.

Thus, with Paul, I can report that I have learned to live and to worship in both poverty and plenty, "to be abased . . . and . . . to abound: . . . to be full and to be hungry . . . I can do all things through Christ which strengtheneth me" (Phil. 4:12-13 KJV).

The Simplicity of God's Word

Why is Christianity so clearly *for* simplicity of life and *opposed to* waste, overconsumption, and luxury? The answer is simple but not easy: Because our faith is based on stewardship of the earth and man's response of gratitude to God.

The plain life has its charter in Genesis:

> Be fruitful and multiply, and fill the earth and subdue it; and have dominion over the fish of the sea and over the birds of the air and over every living thing that moves upon the earth.
>
> (Gen. 1:28 RSV)

Yet within the Old Testament period, two strands of human conduct and belief developed. One strand depicts the growth of man's power with tendency toward luxury; the other is the constant reminder that the simpler life is closer to the ways of God.

The story of man's prideful attempt to master the earth and to exercise lordship over other men, resulting in the growth of great cities, wealthy classes and luxury, is told in the Tower of Babel incident (Genesis 11). This grasping after power and wealth led to deep divisions and mistrust among people, shown in God's confusion of human language and the scattering of people over the earth (Gen. 11:7-9).

But the human desire for wealth and power continued, until it came to its greatest expression in Israel many centuries later under King Solomon (1 Kings 1-11).

Quite clearly the author of 1 Kings shows that Solomon's weakness for luxury, wealth, power, and the sensual pleasures his wealth afforded him, caused the breakdown of the kingdom. Upon Solomon's death, the kingdom was divided into the Northern Kingdom of Israel and the Southern Kingdom of Judah. A kingdom divided loses its strength and, before long, Israel was conquered by surrounding empires.

The author's disapproval of Solomon's love of luxury is plain, although he also expresses pride in Solomon's greatness. The writer reflects the other strand in the Hebrew Scriptures (our Old Testament), the prophetic tradition of the early (non-writing) and classical (writing) prophets. The prophetic tradition stretched back at least to the experiences of the tribe of Israel in the wilderness (after the Exodus) and perhaps as far back as before the sojourn in Egypt to the remote past when Abraham wandered in the deserts of the Middle East. This prophetic tradition also stretched forward through the great eighth-century (BC) prophets to John the Baptist and to Jesus Himself in the first century (AD).

From the standpoint of the prophetic criticism of Israelite religion and life, luxury was sinful. Overconsumption by the few meant lack of food and the necessities of life for the many. Luxury and the acquiring of great wealth equals injustice, according to the prophets—and this is abhorrent to God:

"Therefore because you trample upon the poor

and take from him exactions of wheat,
you have built houses of hewn stone,
    but you shall not dwell in them;
you have planted pleasant vineyards,
    but you shall not drink their wine.
For I know how many are your transgressions,
    and how great are your sins—
you who afflict the righteous, who take a bribe,
    and turn aside the needy in the gate.
"I hate, I despise your feasts,
    and I take no delight in your solemn assemblies.
Even though you offer me your burnt offerings and cereal offer-
        ings,
    I will not accept them,
and the peace offerings of your fatted beasts
    I will not look upon."

(Amos 5:11-12, 21-22 RSV)

Hear this, you who trample upon the needy,
    and bring the poor of the land to an end,
saying, "When will the new moon be over,
    that we may sell grain?
And the sabbath,
    that we may offer wheat for sale,
that we may make the ephah small and the shekel great,
    and deal deceitfully with false balances,
that we may buy the poor for silver
    and the needy for a pair of sandals,
    and sell the refuse of the wheat?"
The Lord has sworn by the pride of Jacob:
    "Surely I will never forget any of their deeds."

(Amos 8:4-7 RSV)

The Prophet's Words Are Still True Today

Amos is a very contemporary book. Its straightforwardness catches our attention and the kind of injustice denounced therein is still prevalent in our time. Without too much difficulty, we can think of a number of parallels between Israel in 750 BC and America in the late twentieth century. The people of North America have not always translated their many special gifts and privileges into special responsibilities toward less fortunate people.

North America's wealth and power is a grace of God, given not only for our own use, but for the benefit of the world. Our society makes much of private property, but frequently does not recognize the inherent responsibilities of ownership as Amos and, later, Jesus Christ pointed them out to us.

Because we have not always been faithful, our inconsistencies are blaring and disheartening. It is well known that the countries of North America embrace a double standard. In his book, *The Other America,* Michael Harrington has forced a confrontation with the "caste system" of the Western world. There is the society of the middle class and the well-to-do, much publicized by television and the press. Then there is "the other America"—a world of poverty where exist the urban ghettoes and isolated rural shacks of literally millions of blacks, Mexican-Americans, Indians, and the poor whites of Appalachia. If Amos were alive today, he would be standing on the Capitol steps in Washington demanding to know why there are so many blighted lives in the richest country on earth!

One of Amos's major thrusts was directed toward sterile religion. Again and again he tried to point out that God values justice done to human beings over ceremonial language and ritual. Today there is a similar, though less vehement, criticism leveled at the church. Some conscientious souls, moved by the plight of the poor, question the expensive stained-glass windows and padded pews added to our sanctuaries to lure the soft, affluent Christians who wish to worship in the same style in which they have become accustomed to living!

Both Judaism and Christianity come to their fulfillment in the loving actions of life, rather than in ceremony and pious language. True worship, says the ever-pragmatic James, takes place in acts of love and helping, not inside the walls of the church.

We know that churches have frequently identified themselves with forces seeking to bring social and economic justice to the blacks, the poor, the young, and others excluded from the benefits of Western society. We must also know that, except for the efforts of a few very dedicated clergy and lay people, support in the churches for such movements has been largely verbal. Great pronouncements without great commitments of self and substance accomplish little. What has been lacking in the church up to now has been a willingness of individuals to risk themselves in the way Amos did. We must recall that our Lord said of the lukewarm Laodiceans, "I will spew you out of my mouth" (Rev. 3:16 RSV).

Applying the Word to Our Generation

In applying Amos' teachings to our day, there is little room for complacency. If we are sensitive, we cannot fail to see the injustices that are a part of our everyday lives in North America. We must look upon the continuation of poverty in our rich society as failure to live fully by the standards of justice. We must look upon the multiplication of churches and institutions and the thousands of ceremonies of worship that apparently usher in no sensitive social conscience as the same type of failure made at the shrine of Bethel, where religion was seen as a support for the state. The Prophet declares that the state and its injustice stand under the judgment of God (see Amos 7:10 ff).

If we search for the meaning of the title *prophet,* we will find that the popular conception of a prophet as one who foretells the future completely misses the point. Rather, prophets are those who have made a deep response to the demands of God upon their lives and who uncompromisingly apply these demands to society.

Is it possible that we have men and women who stand in the prophetic tradition as they live and work in the twentieth century? How can we ignore challenges of leaders of the poor, minority groups, and the disadvantaged as a prophetic call to change before we are destroyed by our selfishness?

Jesus said that before we can truly worship God, we must first put our relationships with man in order. He said, "leave your gift there before the altar and go; first be reconciled to your brother, and then come and offer your gift'' (Matt. 5:24 RSV). Before worship must come reconciliation. Jesus' teaching stands in the prophetic tradition of Amos.

Prophetic Criticism

Amos's most stinging indictment was hurled at the rich and spoiled, who swilled wine and gorged themselves while the poor starved. Amos called the rich women of that day "cows of Bashan," referring to the bulls of Bashan, famous for their loud bellowing. These women lay on their beds and called for more wine. Their husbands were obliged to continue the oppression of the poor to appease their demands. Soon, however, said Amos, the Lord in His wrath would send enemy soldiers to drag them out of the city with the hooks on their spears. The rich would become slaves, eventually to be killed and cast on the refuse heap of Mount Harmon. Luxury gained by taking the livelihood of the poor and powerless, according to the prophet, was the greatest sin against God's covenant.

God cannot be bribed, Amos further declared. The pretense of religion did not ensure that the wealthy would be spared. On the contrary, their trips to the sacred shrines at Bethel and Gilgal were multiplications of their sinfulness.

Amos pictured God as the Creator who not only makes wind and fire, darkness and day—but the One who directs the minds of people. He is Spirit who lives and moves in the events of history. God deeply cares for those who are cheated out of the chance to attain their full measure of maturity in Him. A God of wrath, His anger is but the other side of His love.

Although the people engaged in religious activities, they had no sense of the real presence of God in life. It must have been a frightening thing to hear Amos say, "Prepare to meet your God, O Israel!" (Amos 4:12 RSV). No less is that imperative directed to our perverse generation!

Amos 4:4 has some remarkable parallels to the teachings of

Jesus. Amos makes the point that an outer show of religion is not just useless when separated from true godliness, but it is actually hateful to God. In Mark 7:1-13, Jesus denounced the Pharisees for having that kind of outward, empty religion. "You leave the commandment of God, and hold fast the tradition of men," Jesus says (Mark 7:8 RSV). Jesus called such religious leaders "whitewashed tombs" (Matt. 23:27-28 RSV) who, like *The House of the Seven Gables* in Nathaniel Hawthorne's famous story by that name, are beautifully painted outside, but inside are full of death and decay.

In the same U.S. city where a horse was sold by his owner for $150,000, four malnourished children were bitten by rats in their home. What do you think Amos would have had to say about that? When does my right to have more than I need to live even the most comfortable style of life, while others suffer from want, become a sin? Ask yourself such a question seriously and you will see the prophetic basis for finding your joy in a plainer life style.

Jesus, Friend of the Poor

In the New Testament, the *plain* life is portrayed as the *godly* life by both John the Baptist and the Lord Jesus. John was a Nazarite, living at the edge of the desert on wild food he gathered himself, dressing only in skins and deriding luxury and injustice in the wealthy and ruling families of the land. He opposed power which exacted unjust taxes from the poor. And Jesus Christ supported his beliefs.

> And Jesus said to him, "Foxes have holes, and birds of the air have nests; but the Son of man has nowhere to lay his head."
> (Luke 9:58 RSV)

Even before Jesus' birth, what the Reformed theologian, Jürgen Moltmann of Germany, calls "God's tilt toward the poor and the oppressed" is made clear in Mary's response to the angel, the Magnificat:

> "He has shown strength with his arm,
> he has scattered the proud in the imagination of their hearts,
> he has put down the mighty from their thrones,
> and exalted those of low degree;
> he has filled the hungry with good things,
> and the rich he has sent empty away."
>
> (Luke 1:51-53 RSV)

Paul caught the essence of Jesus' simple, plain, serving life style when he said:

> Have this mind among yourselves, which is yours in Christ Jesus, who, though he was in the form of God, did not count equality with God a thing to be grasped, but emptied himself, taking the form of a servant, being born in the likeness of men. And being found in human form he humbled himself and became obedient unto death, even death on a cross.
>
> (Phil. 2:5-11 RSV)

Paul, too, stresses simplicity of life. So clear is his call for a plain, modest life style on the part of believers that later generations would use Paul as an example of the virtues of monasticism—a complete renunciation of the world. This was, of course, a misuse of Paul's teachings, for he counsels a simple, serving life style *in,* but not *of,* the world. To flee to the deserts or monasteries is to miss the Pauline point that we must live modestly while serving our neighbor in the world. Luther and John Calvin recovered this proper understanding of Paul in their teachings on Christian vocation.

The Word Comes Closer

Amos, so familiar with power politics and economic dishonesty that he seems our contemporary, actually lived 2,800 years ago. His denunciations of selfishness and oppression tell us that the human heart, apart from justification by God's grace in Christ, has changed little over the centuries. Two thousand years of change and experience have gone by since our Lord and the apostle Paul proclaimed that joyful communion that can be ours through the faith that issues in loving relationships. But history's pages are not blank. Christians have many times sought to make the simple gospel of the loving God the basis for their lives and of a renewed social order.

Briefly, some developments in the plain life of believers include both ups and downs, both acts of generosity and deeds of selfishness. We have much to learn from those who came to Christ before us.

The long period of time from the early church (30-312 AD) to the Reformation of Martin Luther (1517 AD) saw both the strands of the Old Testament story—the rise of luxury and power, and the proclamation of prophetic humility and simplicity—developing in the Christian church.

The legalization of the faith under the Emperor Constantine (312 AD) ushered in a period of growing affluence for the clergy which culminated in the claims of the bishops of Rome (the popes) to be set over kings and emperors. Some of the popes were able to make this power effective, and one was able to humble an emperor to walk through the snow to Canossa to seek papal forgiveness. By the time of Luther, the papacy and archbishops throughout Europe were wealthy and powerful, while many peasants were poor, indeed. Luther once remarked on the oddity of German pennies that all seemingly grew wings and flew over the Alps to Rome!

An Alternative Vision

But there was another side to medieval Christianity. Thousands of men and women became monks and nuns, giving up all earthly possessions in order to serve God. Much later, monastic reformers like St. Francis of Assisi turned these devoted people to the service of the poor, the imprisoned, and the ill in the world. While some monasteries grew rich from gifts and the unpaid labor of the lay brothers, most of these Christians in the Dark and Middle Ages did truly live simpler lives out of deep religious motives. Unfortunately, the theology of the church and the monks became corrupt, and human religious works were thought to be necessary for salvation. This theological corruption, rather than the clergy's wealth, first inspired Martin Luther's call for reform.

Luther, too, had been a monk, but had found no comfort in the works righteousness he was taught. In his famous tower experience, Luther found, in St. Paul's Epistle to the Romans, the answer to his spiritual distress. Paul's clear teaching of the gospel states: "By grace you have been saved through faith; and this is not of your own doing, it is the gift of God" (Eph. 2:8 RSV). Once Luther wrote of this evangelical insight, millions all over Germany responded in the Reformation of the church. The Reformation spread quickly.

In his teachings, Luther, followed later by Ulrich Zwingli and John Calvin, recovered the prophetic tradition of the Old Testament, John the Baptist, and Jesus. Luther attacked the sixteenth-century papacy for its luxury and injustice. He attacked the monastic system, also, saying that every Christian has a vocation, a call of God, to serve God and man *in* the world. From his concept of the Christian's calling or vocation, Luther strove to restore the idea of humankind's stewardship under God. We are to work at whatever trade or service is set before us for the good we can do for others and for the glory of God. We are to seek humble service to one another over wealth and luxury. God blesses every vocation, from housewife to shoemaker to soldier. Luther called people back to Paul's words: Remain at your stations; stick to your posts; live simple, inoffensive lives.

The Reformation reminded the church of the sixteenth century that the simple life of faith and sharing with others in love was to be followed by all Christians, lay as well as clergy. Luther knew that joy comes to us when we know Christ and share Him—and ourselves and our goods—with other people.

The Liberation of the Laity

No religious movement ever remains at white heat. The fires of the Reformation died down over the next several centuries. Luxury and worldliness were not overcome in Lutheran, Reformed, Anabaptist, or Roman Catholic churches. But the prophetic notions of simplicity were not lost.

Among the Lutheran and Reformed churches, the Pietist movement developed; and among the Anglicans and the Presbyterians, the Puritan movement arose. In Catholicism, a renewed monastic movement continued. Medieval Catholicism contributed much to the ideals of Christian simplicity. The guides for the conduct of the lives of lay men and women which were a part of the later Protestant plainness had originally been teachings for monks. Calvin echoed Luther's teaching that lay persons as well as clergy have a calling from God. The Pilgrims brought that belief to America. The Protestant ideal of these Pilgrims became a kind of lay monasticism, in which one served God and the world *in the world*. Our Protestant ethic of hard work and frugality is based on this ideal. No doubt this ideal is true and good, but unfortunately, it has often been corrupted to mean that we only find our worth as persons in our work and possessions.

During the Reformation, some Christians thought Luther in Germany and Zwingli in Switzerland had not gone far enough. At Zurich, in the 1520s, these people, called Anabaptists, dissented from the Reformed Church. They called themselves the Swiss Brethren, although we know them as the Mennonite Church. While there were theological differences concerning the separation of church and state and the practice of baptism, questions of personal and church discipline were paramount issues.

Ultimately, a Swiss Bishop, Jacob Amman, split away from the Mennonites over the Ban, the issue of strictness in disciplining believers. The Amish, the plainest of the Plain People, were then formed. Soon after the split, many Mennonites and the Amish emigrated to America, to William Penn's tolerant colony of Pennsylvania. The Mennonites made their first permanent settlement at Germantown, Pennsylvania, in 1683.

While the theology and strict discipline of church members among the Amish, and to a slightly lesser extent among the Mennonites, may not be to the liking of most Protestant Americans, the plain life style of these radical Christians has always been respected. The lessons we can learn from the plain people are even more coveted today, when we are finally learning that luxury cannot give happiness and the resources of the earth are limited.

We should look again at the life styles and beliefs of the Brethren, Mennonites, and Amish. They do not pollute the earth. They do not waste food. They concentrate on the care of the earth and the care of their families. They have no ambitions for wealth or status. They harbor no political lusts to control the lives of their neighbors. All they ask for is the right to live simple, godly lives. The joy of these plain people lies in their communion with Christ and with one another. Contemporary Evangelical Christians have *much* to learn from these Bible-believers, who see the gospel as a pattern for a simple life of love, peace, service, and joy.

Unfortunately, the Evangelical movement today, directed by well-dressed, well-financed leaders, speaking and singing from huge auditoriums, seems to reek of success and self-satisfaction with American materialism. "Love God and He will take good care of you," is the gospel proclaimed from many of these platforms. We rarely hear and rarely live the great theme of sanctification, "Love God and devote your life to loving, as He does, the least of these." In our material abundance we have been able to build luxurious church buildings and provide fabulous financial support for revivalists and musical groups, and still have something left to give to missions and the poor—but the percentage has been overwhelmingly in favor of what we enjoy, not in favor of those in need.

Kurt Vonnegut, the contemporary novelist, preached the 1980 Palm Sunday sermon for an Episcopal church in Manhattan.

Vonnegut, well known for his searing criticism of modern society, criticized the people of Jesus' day for not recognizing who Jesus was and is. He observed wryly, "You can trust a crowd to look at the wrong end of a miracle every time."

When we survey nearly 2,000 years of Christian history, Vonnegut's observation begins to make sense. Comparing the poor Man, Jesus, who died as an outcast, with the luxury and comfort of American Christians, we must exclaim: "We look at the wrong end of a miracle every time!"

The Plain People have something to teach us. Let us listen to what the Spirit may be saying to the churches of our time.

LIVING THE JOY

Eastminster Presbyterian Church

In early 1976, Eastminster Presbyterian Church in suburban Wichita, Kansas, had an ambitious—and expensive—church construction program in the works. Their architect had prepared a $525,000 church building program. Then a devastating earthquake struck in Guatemala on February 4, destroying thousands of homes and buildings. Many evangelical congregations lost their church buildings.

When Eastminster's board of elders met shortly after the Guatemalan tragedy, a layman posed a simple question: "How can we set out to buy an ecclesiastical Cadillac when our brothers and sisters in Guatemala have just lost their little Volkswagen?"

An Ecclesiastical Cadillac Or A Guatemalen Volkswagen?

The elders courageously opted for a dramatic change of plans. They slashed their building program by nearly two-thirds and settled instead on church construction costing $180,000. Then they sent their pastor and two elders to Guatemala to see how they could help. When the three returned and reported tremendous need, the church borrowed $120,000 from a local bank and rebuilt 26 Guatemalan churches and 28 Guatemalan pastors' houses . . .

Eastminster stays in close touch with the church in Central America and has recently pledged $40,000 to an evangelical seminary there. The last few years have seen tremendous growth—in spiritual vitality, concern for missions and even in attendance and budget. Dr. [Frank] Kick [Eastminster's pastor] believes that cutting their building program to share with needy sisters and brothers in Guatemala "meant far more to Eastminster Presbyterian than to Guatemala."

Attendance, Budget Increase Dramatically

In the past seven years, Sunday worship average attendance has increased from 286 to 750, and Sunday School attendance, from 50 to 460. Seven years ago, Eastminster's missions budget was $6,000 ("if there was any left over," says Dr. Kick); currently, it is $235,000 ("Guaranteed!").

In the fall of 1980, the church, still painfully in need of building space, brought before the church another building plan. And again, the church voted to forego their "ecclesiastical Cadillac" and devote the entire building funds to missions. On the spot, they increased their missions budget from $101,000 to $235,000, again postponing their dream of a church adequate in size for the rapidly growing congregation.

And again, miraculous growth took place.

Though still lacking adequate space, the membership of the church is convinced that the right decision was made and that the church has been tremendously blessed.

Eastminster, says Dr. Kick, has had no problem with the local missions budget, with 46 percent presently funnelled into the mission field. But their ambitions are still higher. The goal for missions is 100 percent of their total income.

"Show me a church with a concern for others," emphasizes Dr. Kick, "and I'll show you a church with an active missions program."

The Eastminster Presbyterian congregation asked the right questions. They asked whether their building program was justified at this moment in history given the particular needs of the body of Christ worldwide and the mission of the church in the world. The question was not: Are gothic (or glass) cathedrals ever legitimate? It was rather: Is it right to spend $3.9 billion (in 1970 dollars) on church construction, when over 2.5 billion people have not yet heard of Jesus Christ and when one billion people are starving or malnourished?

Since March 1, 1981, EASTMINSTER PRESBYTERIAN CHURCH, Wichita, Kansas, having donated a large percentage of budget funds to missions, has scheduled three morning services and two Sunday School sessions because of phenomenal growth. Portions of this account appeared originally in Christianity Today, *August 17, 1979.*

7
THE JOY OF A RADICAL LIFE STYLE

Sven and his family are attractive folk of Norwegian heritage. They live in Saskatchewan, on the Canadian prairies. Tall, lean and Nordic blond, Sven's family of four lives a comfortable life while he completes his studies for the Lutheran ministry. Seminary students are a notoriously poor lot, but Sven's belief in thrift and reclamation gives his family a good life.

Sven's house is full of beautiful things, many of them scrounged from the local dump or bartered in exchange for labor. An auto which he earned by landscaping a neighbor's yard stands outside his house. The back yard is neatly packed with 3,000 bricks, three large stacks of lumber, and other supplies for future additions to the house. This material was picked up on trash piles at construction sites or where buildings had been demolished.

"It's a shame what people throw away," Sven observes. "Why, a furniture truck pulled up to the dump one day and discarded two tables with broken legs. There were five good legs between the two, so I put together one sound table on the spot."

Sven's family enjoys the plain life with taste and style. Paint and hard work turn old items into useful, even beautiful ones. Seasonings make the simplest food tasty.

Sven and his family are living demonstrations that one can live a simple, but very cultured life on a small budget. What it takes is a devotion to preserving natural resources, to making maximum use of everything (no waste), and a lot of hard work. These are all Christian attitudes and actions, although they may seem *radical* to many people. And that's the point. Being radical in our commitment to Christ and to our neighbor may well be our calling as Christians.

Toward A Deeper Understanding

The Christian life is not and has never been a simple, straightforward thing. It is full of surprises, tensions, and problems. A moment's reflection will erase any lingering ideas that it is easy to make Christian judgments or plan a Christian policy or life style.

Jesus' problematical approach to life disturbed many of the religious people of His time. The Pharisees couldn't understand why He associated openly with sinners like tax collectors and harlots. Jesus' reply was not to defend the sin, but to express compassion for the sinner: "I came not to call the righteous, but sinners" (Matt. 8:13 RSV).

Expecting The End

The tension grew after Jesus' Resurrection and Ascension. The early disciples expected the Final Judgment to come quickly. Paul's early letters reflect his haste to carry the gospel far and wide. Paul's counsel was for Christians to keep themselves untangled from the world and worldly responsibilities. But it soon became clear that the early church hadn't listened clearly to its Lord. The Last Judgment was sure, but not necessarily close at hand in time. The church, if it were to perform its mission for an undetermined time, must have some policy for dealing with the world.

In this context, the question of the most appropriate Christian life style became acute. Should Christians mingle in the world or should they remain aloof? There were various answers then as there are now. Those who wished to withdraw from the world and its ways became monks and nuns. In time, monasticism became a major feature of Christendom. But other Christians, perhaps the majority, chose another option. If God created the world and called it good, then sent His Son to redeem the lost and sinful, they felt constrained to stay in contact with the world. Ultimately, while some sought out the monasteries, the majority of Christians lived in the world, becoming more or less indistinguishable from the rest of society. Such was the situation when Luther's Reformation shook Western Christendom to its roots. Among the folk who responded to the call to cleanse Christianity were a group of Dutch, German, and Swiss peasants, whose descendants became the Plain People of contemporary Pennsylvania, Ohio, and the Midwestern areas of the U.S. and Canada.

Simple Experiments in America

America has a long history of Christian experiments with the plain life, beyond those of the Amish and Mennonites. Many other pietistic groups were founded, flourished and died here. The Shakers are one of these unique groups.

"The United Society of Believers in Christ's Second Coming" or the "Millenial Church" was the official name of the Shakers, who were called "Shaking Quakers" because of a peculiar dance they practiced. Mother Ann Lee Stanley brought the sect to America from England in 1774. Shaker settlements—now long abandoned—are preserved as state historical sites in Kentucky and elsewhere.

The Shakers had a built-in failure factor. Mother Ann believed that sexual relations were the root of all sin, hence the group was celibate. It could only exist by conversions and was doomed to die out.

The Shakers formed communities apart from the world. These villages abundantly satisfied the basic needs of life and became creative centers of architecture, furniture construction, cattle raising, gardening, and farming.

German simple life groups arrived early in America. The Hutterites or German Anabaptists established colonies that are thriving to this day in the United States and Canada. The Ephrata Community formed in Pennsylvania. George Rapp (1757-1847) established "Harmony" colony in the same state in 1804. In 1815, this group branched out and founded "New Harmony" in Indiana and "Economy" in Ohio. "The Amana Society" or "Community of True Inspiration" was founded in 1943 at Ebenezer, near Buffalo, New York. In 1850 they moved to Iowa, where the Amana Society has prospered as an incorporated cooperative since 1932. Most of us have heard of—or purchased—household products bearing this brand name.

Others sought the plain life in an earthly utopia. Such were the followers of John Humphrey Noyes (1811-1886). Noyes was convinced the Second Coming had already occurred, and preached perfectionism in the form of socialism. Later he declared the establishment of the kingdom of God on earth, and instituted communal sex, or free love. This brought many problems and the group disbanded in 1879.

Of course, no account of the desire for a plainer life is complete without mentioning Joseph Smith and the Church of Latter-Day Saints, or Mormons. Mormonism began in the same social matrix of millenial fervor and the quest for full spiritual perfection, of the previously mentioned groups. In 1827, when Smith claimed to have discovered the hidden "Book of Mormon," upper New York State was called "The Burned-Over District," because so many revivals had been held there that the population was spiritually exhausted and confused. In 1844

Smith led the group to Illinois where he was murdered. The Mormons moved on to Independence, Missouri, where some settled, but the bulk of the "saints" pushed on to Utah under the leadership of Brigham Young. Their settlement of that far western territory is an American saga.

In time, the central focus of Mormonism was clarified as the family. After polygamy was abolished to conform to U.S. law, the church stressed the values of the monogamous family. Today, in accord with its pioneer ideals, the Latter-Day Saints Church urges each member family to store a year's supply of food and encourages the local church and every family to make themselves as self-sufficient as possible. It is not unusual to see part of the property of a Mormon meeting house devoted to a congregational garden. Recently, while visiting a Mormon home, I discovered the family had, among other supplies, 3,000 pounds of "wheat berries" stored in the basement. If trouble comes, the wife plans to grind these berries into flour with a hand-cranked mill. The plain-life vision is alive today among the Mormons.

From this description of the several simple life movements in America, we can see that the healthy impulse to simpler living can be contaminated by other ideas. Several of these movements are heretical by any standard of orthodoxy.

Most were, or are communistic in their social outlook. Some have practiced what the rest of us would call immorality. Consequently, it is a good thing "to have your faith on straight" and to be aware of some less than Christian ideas in the thought-world of simpler living. To this end, it is necessary to consider a biblical theology of the plain life.

Plain People Reassessed

The contemporary movement toward a plainer life owes something to the historic plain people movements in Christianity, especially to their American expressions in the Amish, Mennonites, Hutterites, and Shakers. Yet the influence is more one of historic justification or support than of direct influence. The reasons for that are varied but clear. First there is sufficient basis for the plain life in the Gospels themselves.

Secondly, the return to plain principles had a great social background in general American life less than a half-century ago. There is nothing strange about thrift and reliance upon responsible interdependence with our neighbors.

But most clearly so many of the theological, philosophical, and economic principles or plain-people experiments in America are out of harmony both with a general evangelical outlook and with the philosophies of our time. For example, the Shakers were celibate communists. Their religious ideals were odd and heretical even in their day. Hutterites practice a form of communalism and the clannishness and extreme conservatism of the Amish are not attractive models for Christians today.

For all these reasons, it is obvious that contemporary plain people are not trying to imitate the historic Plain People of Christendom in any precise way. Yet there are things we can learn from the older plain living groups, even the Shakers, the most extreme of these groups. The Shakers glorified manual labor. They saw work with the hands as good for the soul and for the community, as it subjugated lust, taught humility, created order and a surplus of wealth to use for charity, and built up the fellowship. The true idea of a holy people, Mother Ann Lee taught, is one in which spiritual sentiments are supported by domestic labors.

As I spend my free days sanding rust off the used Scout II four-wheel drive vehicle I bought to haul wood and groceries during the wintertime, and talk to my friend John Kilpatrick, I appreciate the fellowship and spiritual values in manual labor. We save more than the amount of the bills for mechanical and body work when we do those jobs ourselves. We save a part of ourselves—a basic way of being human—that so many of us have lost in this affluent, over-specialized world. There is a tonic for the soul in the simple task of being independent, able to do for oneself and for others. The devil can't use busy hands. We can overlook those ideas of the older plain people that don't fit our situation, and still learn much from them.

For Everything There Is A Season

The rise of a highly technological economic system in the twentieth century made luxury a possibility for many people in the West. This system, spread over North America, Western Europe, and Japan, is now called into question and threatened by the energy crisis; the economic and political problems that oil-producing countries now give the developed countries. There is thus a real-world, pragmatic reason why North Americans and Europeans may now listen to the thrift-oriented, responsible stewardship taught by the Christian tradition. Today, many Christians are looking for the freedom from things and the elevation above worry about resources and money that plain-living Christians have enjoyed in every age. With the Catholic theologian, Karl Rahner, we are learning again that grace is found in everyday, ordinary human life. With the great doctor of the Church, Thomas Aquinas, we have come to see that grace completes nature; it does not destroy it. God's grace is given us for life together, sharing and loving, here in this world. With Luther we pray to stay at our posts, building and working, until God's kingdom comes, for we know that the kingdom comes in God's time, not ours. With the modern theologian, Reinhold Niebuhr, we are now ready to look for "common grace," the opportunities for joy and service that meet us in our everyday lives.

The Theology of the Plain Life

"The Plain Life" aims at freeing people from the tension, anxiety, and rush of modern life. Many of these alternatives include moving to small towns or rural areas, with the giving up of corporate jobs and high standards of living. "Plain People" often farm, or at least garden, so as to get back to the soil and in touch with nature.

While many of the persons who are turning toward a simpler life do not have clear religious convictions for doing so, many others do. And, in the case of the less obviously religious, they often have vague, but real, beliefs that point towards religious doctrines. These doctrines include Christian teachings concerning the Creation, the Incarnation, the dignity of man as the child of God, and the presence of the Spirit in the world. Taken together, this outlook might be called the theology of the plain life.

Creation

The plain person views the world as originally good though it is now badly corrupted. "And God saw that it was good" (Gen. 1:10 NIV). The fact that the air over our cities and the waters of many of our rivers are soiled and polluted to the extreme only make the plain person sad and angry—for he knows the physical world was, and can again be, good. Many plain people affirm that man is responsible to God for this misuse of His creation. The world was created to be used by man, but in a healthy, non-exploitative way that would preserve its goodness. Mankind as a total race, is now guilty for the way in which this responsibility has been abused. The abuse of power seen in the Watergate case are as nothing compared to the misuse of the gifts, offices, opportunities and powers given us by the Creator, God. All of us have fallen short. No wonder the world has been polluted and its resources plundered.

Man

The plain person affirms the dignity of man. As much anger as plain people feel over the abuse of the environment, they feel more over the exploitation of man by man. The dehumanization of the urban dweller and the industrial worker is the precise reason many plain people move to rural areas and seek to earn their living by cooperation with nature and each other.

Incarnation

Man's dignity is inherent in the fact that he was created in the image of God. Plain people accept this kinship to the God of Creation, as well as to the Lord of history, the Older Brother, Jesus Christ. Jesus' call to men to love one another, trust in God, and give up the desire to enrich themselves at the expense of others, inspires plain people to accept Him as model and guide. Of course, to emphasize the goodness of Creation is to make possible belief in God's manifestation of Himself in history (the Incarnation).

For Christian plain people, the world, despite its polluted aspect, is the kind of place where God can be in the midst of human life. Jesus Christ is God come in the flesh. The world He graced is good. This distinctive belief that Jesus is not merely a model for a "good life," but is actually the only true God come in the flesh, distinguishes the Christian plain person from all other, humanistically inclined followers of a simpler life.

The Spirit

Jesus taught men to trust in God and love one's neighbor as himself. Like Jesus, the plain person of today affirms that the secrets of happiness, wholeness, and blessing lie not in the accumulation of things, but in the building of spiritual treasures (see Matt. 6:19-20). The person who turns away from the business success ladder toward a simpler, more human life, believes—as did Socrates of Athens and Jesus—in the development of our inner life of communion with God instead of seeking wealth and worldly honors.

Such a life of inwardness and the cultivation of human relationships is called "walking in the Spirit" by Paul in Galatians. We learn, in a simpler life, to become indifferent toward outward circumstances, to become inwardly sufficient, and above all, to discern the unseen presence of the Spirit in the world. In such inwardness, by such a walk with and in the Spirit, we can become (in Luther's phrase) "little Christs" to our fellowmen. Our spiritual development is not for ourselves alone, but for our brothers and sisters everywhere.

Sharers and Conservers

These reflections upon the plain life show the solid theology that lies behind these unusual (for the twentieth century) forms of thought and action. There is a depth and maturity of great theological dimensions behind the plain life, and the joys of such plain living can make a loving life possible, so that the plain person can become a sharer and conserver, and not a mere user and consumer of the elements of God's beautiful world.

Reflections on Sins Against Planet Earth

Environmental degradation is denounced from all sides in the 1980s, with even giant corporations printing pious phrases about the protection of the air, earth, and water. Ministers and lay Christians speak out against pollution, Sunday school lessons make reference to it, and vacation church schools clean up the surrounding lawns. But most of the rhetoric used by secular and church people comes from the evangelical biologists and other natural scientists who first promoted the ecological crisis. A theology of the plain life must go beyond references to exploitation. We must call exploitation by its proper names—selfishness, self-destruction, sin. The question of the value man puts upon the material world is as old as philosophy, and even older, for it goes back to the Hebrews' reflections upon their Genesis experiences with God. Obviously, the world contains elements that build up and those that degrade. Things grow and die, are born and decline, wear out and refresh themselves.

Man, too, is a part of the natural order and he exhibits the same polarity of positivity and negativity. Man builds and destroys, sins and repents, befriends his fellows and declares war upon them. The beauty of the underbrush may conceal deadly serpents; the smiling face may be a ruse to lure us into an ambush. What are we to believe about the world—including man? The biblical fathers wrestled with problems like these. Certainly they took their own experiences very seriously. We must see that there is an empirical, an experiential, basis to much of the biblical message.

The Bible is about real people, and was written by real people. The mode in which much of the earlier Old Testament material is written is not a lack of realism but an attempt to state universal insights in a manner men of every time can understand. God made the world, not just a part of it, but all of it. And he made it from nothing; called it into being of His own will—not out of any pre-existing matter. That is the declaration of Genesis—and it means the world is good, since He who made it is good. The Bible makes no differentiation between spirit and matter as is made in Greek thought. The Greek philosophers, especially Plato, thought that the material world was basically evil. The tragedy of world history, man's inhumanity to man, and his careless exploitation of the environment, thus was explained to the Greeks as a consequence of the evil infecting the world. This theological outlook is known as Dualism, and rests on a view of God as less than the Supreme Lord of the Universe. Such a basic Dualism was not agreeable to the Hebrew faith. Therefore, all simple explanations that depreciate the material world and the physical body of man are rejected by biblical theology. Regardless of whatever else is true about the nature of the world since man's "fall," it is not evil, but damaged by man's selfish willfulness. This is the message of Genesis 3 and of Paul's insight in Romans 8, that the entire creation groans as it awaits the redemption of the children of God.

The history of Christianity has been an admixture of the assertion of the goodness of matter and the Greek Dualistic outlook. Monasticism, celibacy, fasting—all these age-old practices grew out of the Greek world-view. These Platonic ideas about the essential evil of the flesh stand behind the twisted history of human sexuality in the West. Over the past fifty years we have lived through a sexual revolution that owes as much to the recovery of the biblical conception of the goodness of the flesh as it does to other, more negative, elements. Nothing about bodily existence is evil except for the evil use we make of it, because of our sin. The person attracted to the plain life believes in the goodness of nature. The artificiality of technologies and social customs designed to separate us from nature and from our own bodies and their impulses are rejected by the plain people. The theory of the plain life, though on healthy ground, may go too far towards optimism if it neglects the equally biblical idea of sin. Though basically good, man and the world are afflicted by the "fall." The "fall" concept means that there is a tragic flaw in man—and through him a tragic element in the world. But this is the fault of man, not of the plan of God. When we are convinced of the detrimental effects of our technological culture, it is far too easy to consider a non-technological, simpler life as wholly healthy, wholly good.

Unfortunately such a simplistic assessment won't hold water. Modern technological society is not wholly detrimental, nor is a simple life wholly good. Medical technology, so badly lacking in primitive areas, will show the truth of this insight. Sin and consequent accidents, illness, war, and death must remind us of the tragic elements in life and the world. Going back to a simpler, agricultural life will not change that—although we might reduce some of the demonic nature of social life.

My oldest son loved the sunrises we saw when hiking through the Mexican desert, but feared the snakes, scorpions, and spiders. We must be careful not to be overly romantic so that we worship nature. It is nature's God, our God, who is the Lord.

Not To Live Simply Could Be Sinful

Professor Alan Johnson of Wheaton College has recently challenged Evangelical Christians to come to a full biblical understanding of sin (in *United Evangelical Action,* Spring, 1980). Johnson points out our common misunderstanding of sin, saying:

In the first place, our understanding of sin comes from a mixture of biblical, societal, and ecclestiastical traditions which are often difficult to sort out . . . Secondly, our sociological position affects the way we see both reality and sin. A Christian who lives among the poor, for example, will have a somewhat different understanding of sin from the rich, upper-class Christian.

Johnson reviews the biblical data and concludes:

Basically, then, sin is religious. It is a rebellion against God, an effort to usurp the place of God, an alienation from God, a transgression of the divinely revealed will . . . But sin is also moral, a failure of love and loving—justice in our relations with others, a willful disregard or sacrifice of others: for the welfare or satisfaction of the self.

In his conclusion Johnson specifies one

issue which can affect today's evangelicals' relationship with God and one another . . . Has the cult of prosperity deceived us as it has others in times past? Sodom's greater sin was not sexual perversion but, like Babylon's—the mother of harlots—it was pride and failure to love and compassion in sharing its wealth with the poor and needy (Ezek. 16:39, 40; Rev. 3, 7, 17). The attitude that "it's mine, I own it" is a perversion of the biblical authorization of private ownership. Scripture declares that the Lord is owner of all.

He summarizes:

The recovery of the biblical concept of sin is absolutely imperative if evangelicals are to preserve the original power and meaning of the Gospel.

The concepts of God, man, Christ, church, sin, salvation, and hope for the future are major elements in any Christian theology. For the plain person who is also an Evangelical Christian, all of these concepts are living realities. The desire to seek out a simpler life is not based on a Pantheism, a belief that the world itself is God, nor on a Pelagian theology, the false belief that mankind has not been corrupted by sin.

Though plainness has often been associated with separatism and sectarianism in Christian history, it need not result in the feeling that we must separate ourselves from the world. We may well continue to live in our communities and worship in our congregations. Plainness is basically a matter of the heart and of attitudes, and may be expressed in our behavior in limited or more radical ways. Christian plain people take sin very seriously and see salvation as obtainable through faith in the person and work of Jesus Christ.

Clearly, living a plainer life is not a "good work" in the sense of meriting God's favor. It is not necessary to give up anything in order to earn salvation. We are justified by faith alone, without works. So plainness is not a part of justification. Yet plainness has a theological dimension—sanctification.

Sanctification is the process whereby the forgiven sinner grows more and more in the likeness of Christ, in grace and in personal holiness. Here the adoption of a plainer life style finds its true theological and philosophical significance.

Not to save ourselves, but to surrender ourselves even more fully to Jesus Christ, we try to lay aside and strip away all that hinders our communion with Him and our service to others. The degree of simplicity sought and attained by various people differs widely. For some persons, use of an automobile may compromise their deep beliefs about air pollution or luxury, so they will give up autos; for others, such a sacrifice may seem unnecessary. Here tolerance must be our guide.

> "All things are lawful," but not all things are helpful. "All things are lawful," but not all things build up. Let no one seek his own good, but the good of his neighbor . . . "For the earth is the Lord's and everything in it." If one of the unbelievers invites you to dinner and you are disposed to go, eat whatever is set before you without raising any question on the ground of conscience. For why should my liberty be determined by another man's scruples? If I

partake with thankfulness, why am I denounced because of that for which I give thanks?

So, whether you eat or drink, or whatever you do, do all to the glory of God. Give no offense to Jews or to Greeks or to the church of God.

(1 Cor. 10:23-24, 26-29, 31-32 RSV)

Common Sense

Devotion to a simpler life does not mean that we need go barefoot, live without heat, or become vegetarians. Common sense must be part of our plainer outlook. Yet the term "common sense" is often used as if its meaning were obvious. It may well be neither common nor sensible, but rather, in its Christian expression, a form of "discernment of the spirit." While such discernment is vitally important in all areas of our lives, the area of plainness is most especially so because of the many "fads" that periodically sweep America. A questioning spirit toward fads and fashions that will lure us from the Christian life and waste our goods in the bargain is a good sign of "common sense."

Radical Means Returning to our Roots

The word *radical* is mistrusted by many Christians because of its overuse and abuse in the 1960s. Actually, when correctly used, there is nothing negative about the term or the viewpoint it represents. *Radical* comes from the Latin word *radix,* meaning "roots." Being a *radical* Christian and *radically* changing our life style means returning to our Christian roots—to Jesus Christ and Communion with God through Him. Such a redirection of our lives will also radically change our relationship with our brothers and sisters too. Suddenly, we will find that being one with the Lord makes us one with other people.

We will be radical, but not *fanatical* Christians, living a plain life of joy. A fanatic is the kind of negative person we often mean to point out when we misuse the word, *radical*. A fanatic is self-righteous, so absolutely sure of the superiority of his position that he feels it right to attempt to *force* his beliefs and life style on other people. We are *not* advocating such a self-righteous, intolerant attitude towards either fellow Christians or toward people outside the church. Knowing that plain people are radical but not fanatical is part of the common sense we need in these times that demand changes towards thrift and sharing, but not toward self-righteousness.

The Lure of the Cults

Another area of need for such discernment is in the Christian's response to personalities and groups who claim to offer alternative life styles. These persons and groups are distinguished by their criticism of the present-day materialistic and capitalistic North American culture.

The idealism of youth makes them particularly vulnerable to cult leaders. The quest for a simpler life, for an alternative life style, is a strong element in cult propaganda. Sharing *Christian* information about possible Christian alternatives to cultural conformity may be a real way to combat the growing menace of cult groups.

Since the idealistic young—and older—are drawn to the plain life, it is well to clearly state some of the reliable marks of a *cult* (that is, demonic) leader and cult groups. Not surprisingly, the marks of these deviant approaches to a different life style involve misuses of one's human dignity and demands upon one's money and labor.

Cult groups with one dominant leader may give every evidence of being Christian, or at least religious. On further examination, it may be found that the words and books of the cult leaders are said to be the *only* reliable interpretation of the Scriptures. Many cult leaders claim their leadings to be superior to Scripture, which gives us a real clue as to their true spirit.

The teachings of the Bible are *subtly* perverted to stress the authority and correctness of the cult's teachings. The experience of the early church in Acts 4:32-37, where "no one said that any of the things which he possessed was his own, but they had everything in common'' (v. 32, RSV) may be stressed to make the new member conform to common ownership of goods.

Ultimately, as the experiences of many deceived people testify, all monies are controlled by the cult leader. After the tragedy at Jonestown, for example, hundreds of Social Security checks, cash, and other valuables were found in a trunk in Jim Jones' possession, proving the exploitation of cult members, financially and personally.

Even worse than the cooption of all that a member possesses, or that he can beg, borrow and earn, is the psychological manipulation of the member to make him totally submissive to the leader. Then the deceived person is directed to practice ''heavenly deception'' on others, so as to constantly bring more money into the group. Cults, ultimately, are vehicles for the economic exploitation of idealistic people who join, and of the public which is systematically deceived. We must beware of such groups and leaders, for we did not learn such things in Christ!

All that we need is ours in Christ, and in His church, if we are open to receive it. The young person will find it far better to study the spiritual literature of Christianity than that of other religions and to live by the suggestions of the Mennonite Central Committee (See Appendix), than to lock ourselves into the mind-control of a cult group. The Ten Commandments and the Law of Love are sufficient discipline. Our lives can be simple, peaceful, relaxed, and happy in the faith into which most of us were so blessed as to be born. Before listening to other teachers, we need to listen to what the Spirit of Christ is saying to the churches— and to us.

A Sober Reflection

Adam and Eve tended trees, as did the prophet Amos. God called Abram to a nomadic life of wandering through the deserts. Jesus was a carpenter and lived with fisherfolk and farmers. His few earthly possessions were worn on His back, and hardly compensated the soldiers for the time they spent in crucifying Him. Saul, who became Paul, was pleased to preach the gospel free of charge by supporting his mission with his own hands. The folk who heard the message of Paul and Peter, James and John were simple people, too. Christianity began among slaves in Rome, displaced Jews in Greek cities, common sailors, or traders.

Throughout our history, the faith of the cross has been kept alive at mothers' knees in peasant cottages, African huts, and sod houses on the prairies. Men and women have sung of Jesus' love and God's mighty acts in slave quarters. Fatigued and frightened soldiers have heard of God's mercy from chaplains on a thousand battlefields, and the aged are still warmed by the words of Scripture, "Blessed are the poor in spirit . . . Blessed are the pure in heart" (Matt. 5:3, 8 RSV). The comforting words of Jesus ring down through the ages to the Last Judgment itself.

Why then should anyone think it strange to live a plainer life today?

LIVING THE JOY

John the Baptist

> The word of God came to John son of Zechariah in the desert. So John went throughout the whole territory of the Jordan River, preaching, "Turn away from your sins and be baptized, and God will forgive your sins." As it is written in the book of the prophet Isaiah:
>
> "Someone is shouting in the
>   desert:
> 'Get the road ready for the lord;
> make a straight path for him to travel!

Every valley must be filled up,
  every hill and mountain leveled off.
The winding roads must be made straight,
  and the rough paths made smooth.
All mankind will see God's salvation!' "

**Strange Clothes
And Stranger
Food**

John's clothes were made of camel's hair; he wore a leather belt around his waist, and his food was locusts and wild honey. People came to him from Jerusalem, from the whole province of Judea, and from all over the country near the Jordan River.

Crowds of people came out to John to be baptized by him. "You snakes!" he said to them. "Who told you that you could escape from the punishment God is about to send? Do those things that will show that you have turned from your sins. And don't start saying among yourselves that Abraham is your ancestor. I tell you that God can take these rocks and make descendants for Abraham! The ax is ready to cut down the trees at the roots; every tree that does not bear good fruit will be cut down and thrown in the fire."

The people asked him, "What are we to do, then?"

He answered, "Whoever has two shirts must give one to the man who has none, and whoever has food must share it."

Some tax collectors came to be baptized, and they asked him, "Teacher, what are we to do?"

"Don't collect more than is legal," he told them.

Some soldiers also asked him, "What about us? What are we to do?"

He said to them, "Don't take money from anyone by force or accuse anyone falsely. Be content with your pay."

People's hopes began to rise, and they began to wonder whether John perhaps might be the Messiah. So John said to all of them, "I baptize you with water, but someone is coming who is much greater than I am. I am not good enough even to untie his sandals. He will baptize you with the Holy Spirit and fire. He has his winnowing shovel with him, to thresh out all the grain and gather the wheat into his barn; but he will burn the chaff in a fire that never goes out.''

In many different ways John preached the Good News to the people and urged them to change their ways. But John reprimanded Governor Herod, because he had married Herodias, his brother's wife, and had done many other evil things.

Criticism of Official

At that time Jesus arrived from Galilee and came to John at the Jordan to be baptized by him. But John tried to make him change his mind. ''I ought to be baptized by you,'' John said, ''and yet you have come to me!''

But Jesus answered him, ''Let it be so for now. For in this way we shall do all that God requires.'' So John agreed.

As soon as Jesus was baptized, he came up out of the water. Then heaven was opened to him, and he saw the Spirit of God coming down like a dove and lighting on him. Then a voice said from heaven, ''This is my own dear Son, with whom I am pleased.''

Put Into Prison

Then Herod did an even worse thing by putting John in prison.

When John's disciples told him about all these things, he called two of them and sent them to the Lord to ask him, ''Are you the one John said was going to come, or should we expect someone else?''

When they came to Jesus, they said ''John the Baptist sent us to ask if you are the one he said was going to come, or should we expect someone else?''

At that very time Jesus healed many people from their sicknesses, diseases, and evil spirits, and gave sight to many blind people. He answered John's messengers, ''Go back and tell John what you have seen and heard: the blind can see, the lame can walk, those who suffer from dreaded skin diseases are made clean, the deaf can hear, the dead are raised to life, and the Good News is preached to the poor. How happy are those who have no doubts about me!''

After John's messengers had left, Jesus began to speak about him to the crowds: "When you went out to John in the desert, what did you expect to see? A blade of grass bending in the wind? What did you go out to see? A man dressed up in fancy clothes? People who dress like that and live in luxury are found in palaces! Tell me, what did you go out to see? A prophet? Yes indeed, but you saw much more than a prophet. For John is the one of whom the scripture says: 'God said, I will send my messenger ahead of you to open the way for you.' I tell you,'' Jesus added, "John is greater than any man who has ever lived. But he who is least in the Kingdom of God is greater than John.''

"What Did You Expect?"

All the people heard him; they and especially the tax collectors were the ones who had obeyed God's righteous demands and had been baptized by John. But the Pharisees and the teachers of the Law rejected God's purpose for themselves and refused to be baptized by John.

Jesus continued, "Now to what can I compare the people of this day? What are they like? They are like children sitting in the marketplace. One group shouts to the other 'We played wedding music for you, but you wouldn't dance! We sang funeral songs, but you wouldn't cry!' John the Baptist came, and he fasted and drank no wine, and you said, 'He has a demon in him!; The Son of Man came, and he ate and drank, and you said, 'Look at this man! He is a glutton and winedrinker, a friend of tax collectors and other outcasts!' God's wisdom, however, is shown to be true by all who accept it.''

Nothing Is Without Criticism

For Herod had earlier ordered John's arrest, and he had him tied up and put in prison He had done this because of Herodias, his brother Philip's wife. For some time John the Baptist had told Herod, "It

isn't right for you to be married to Herodias!''
Herod wanted to kill him, but he was afraid of the
Jewish people, because they considered John to be
a prophet.

On Herod's birthday the daughter of Herodias
danced in front of the whole group. Herod was so
pleased that he promised her, ''I swear that I will
give you anything you ask for!''

At her mother's suggestion she asked him,
''Give me here and now the head of John the Baptist on a plate!''

**The Death of A
"Radical"**

The king was sad but because of the promise he
had made in front of all his guests he gave orders
that her wish be granted. So he had John beheaded
in prison. The head was brought in on a plate and
given to the girl, who took it to her mother. John's
disciples came, carried away his body, and buried
it; then they went and told Jesus.

When Jesus heard the news about John, he left
there in a boat and went to a lonely place by himself.

(Luke 3:2-6; Matt. 3:4-6; Luke 3:7-19; Matt.
3:13-17; Luke 3:20; Luke 7:18-35; Matt. 14:1-12
GNB)

---

*JOHN THE BAPTIST was a first-century trend-
setter. The message he was called to deliver took
precedence over even the basic necessities of life.
Jesus affirmed his life style and his zeal in one of
the greatest tributes ever given to a follower.*

8
THE JOY OF
COMMITMENT
TO CHANGE

At the conclusion of Charles Dickens' great classic, *A Christmas Carol,* Ebenezer Scrooge demonstrates his change of heart by a change of life style. Scrooge moves from selfishness to sharing, pouring out his heart and part of his wealth on Bob Cratchit's needy family.

> He went to church, and walked about the streets, and watched the people hurrying to and fro, and patted children on the head, and questioned beggars, and looked down into the kitchens of houses, and up to the windows, and found that everything could yield him pleasure. He had never dreamed that any walk—that anything—could give him so much happiness.

That change is indicated, even necessary, to our survival and to that of the world's entire population, can no longer be denied. We cannot continue to consume most of the world's food and other raw materials and expect many more generations to exist on this planet. But it is the "how" of change that challenges all caring and rational Christians. In the words of Dr. Elton Trueblood, it is a dilemma to be met by both "warm hearts and clear heads."

If the plainer life is attractive today, it is because many of us have confronted honestly those life-denying qualities of acquisitiveness and greed. Any yet, Christians are called upon to be realistic. Before commending the plain life to others, we must assess the degree of plainness that is most equitable for all.

It's clear that a life style characterized by a constant race to encompass as many material possessions as possible—the same kind of life style that is followed by millions of people in the West—results ultimately in early death. James Johnson tells us this "workaholic" life style is as typical of many Christians as it is of secular people. Yet, there are basic human needs which must be met by material possessions if life is to be as full and meaningful as Christians would like it to be.

An Interesting Proposal

The American Council of Life Insurance reminds us that the very plainest life style might not be something we would deliberately seek out, but for two-thirds of the world's population, there is no option. To live such a simple life, one need only follow these instructions:

1. Remove all the furniture and utensils from your home, except a few old blankets, a table, a chair, and a few pots.

2. Keep only a few old clothes for each family member.

3. Remove all plumbing and cut off electricity.

4. Your food larder should consist of a small sack of sugar, some salt, onions, and a small bowl of chickpeas.

5. Discard all newspapers, magazines, and books.

6. There will, of course, be no television, stereo, or radio.

Ideally the Council suggests that one demolish his home and move into a hut located at least twelve miles from the nearest hospital, where the chief physician has been replaced by a midwife. The Council also points out that all insurance policies must be cancelled. That puts the simple life on a "plain" basis indeed.

When we speak of a plainer and simpler life, we don't mean the nasty, brutal, and short lives that so many of God's children are forced to live.

A Challenging Comparison

Just how nasty, brutal, and short these lives can be, even in a relatively developed third-world country, was brought home to me quite painfully just a few years ago.

In my book, *Religion After Forty,* I suggested that in today's society, many people in mid-life are thinking about changing careers, going back to school, retooling themselves to do the kinds of things they have always wanted to do. Generally, a forty-year-old American's health is good, he has wealth and leisure, and the promise of more than thirty additional years of life in our society.

A gentleman in Djakarta, Indonesia, editor of the Baptist book concern there, heard about my book, *Religion After Forty,* and asked for permission to translate it for use by the church in Indonesia. The publisher agreed, and we sent permission and a copy of the book to Indonesia. After a long period of time, I received an apologetic letter from this gentleman.

In it, he wrote, "When I read that you had written a book called *Religion After Forty,* I misunderstood its content. Here in Indonesia, many people die at the age of forty. So as they approach that age, they usually retire from their jobs and return to the villages of their birth to spend their last months. I was looking for a book that would help people to get their lives together and face up to death, with God's comfort. When I read your book about starting a new career, having a second life after forty, I saw the wide gap between America and Indonesia."

I've tried to keep that letter in mind ever since, as I talk to people from Asia and the third world. God forbid that we should have to enter into a simple life like that! We would not willingly seek it out, but would rather reduce our standard of living in order to raise the standard of living for other peoples of the world.

The Good Life

Helen and Scott Nearing, famous pioneers of the plain life, called the life style they sought "The Good Life." They tell us they left the city and moved to rural Vermont in the midst of the Great Depression for three reasons:

> *The first was economic.* We sought to make a depression-free living, as independent as possible of the commodity and labor markets, which could not be interfered with by employers, whether businessmen, politicians, or educational administrators.
> *The second was hygienic.* We wanted to maintain and improve our health. We knew that the pressures of city life were exacting, and we sought a simple basis of well-being where contact with the earth, and home-grown food, would play a large part.
> *Our third objective was social and ethical.* We desired to liberate and disassociate ourselves, as much as possible, from the cruder forms of exploitation; the plunder of the planet, the slavery of man and beast, the slaughter of men in war, and of animals for food.

Our own reasons may differ widely from those of the Nearings. Vernard Eller, in his book, *The Simple Life,* warns us that:

> the Christian doctrine of the simple life would be simplicity itself, except:
> 1. If we let it get too simple, we won't have the wherewithal for a book.
> 2. The Christian teaching is by nature dialectical.
> 3. The people who are supposed to be following the teaching are human beings.

By dialectical, Eller means that our thinking finds itself pulled in two directions at once. In honesty we find it necessary to give weight and attention to two different, and apparently opposed, poles of thought. Eller has in mind the fact that, for the Christian, the simple life will include a rich inner life of faith and devotion to God. But the Christian life also includes the necessity of outward expression. We cannot think that we are pious if we are addicted to luxuries.

Consequently, we want to be prudent and aim at a more satisfying, more saving, and more sharing life style without holding up impossible ideals. I think we will find that there is much about our current life style that is not only out of harmony with a fair understanding of the Christian life, but that is also strangely unsatisfying to us as human beings. We may recall the stress of contemporary life discussed in earlier chapters. We may suddenly realize that our labor-saving devices and much-discussed leisure time has left us busier and more nervously exhausted than ever. We may find that there is much to give up or change.

A Change of View

What are some of the attractions of a plainer life style? We may briefly list the following:

—The lure of simplicity—the idea that there is more contentment in a slower, simpler way of life.

—The attraction of innocence, harmlessness, and peacefulness that is associated with the figures of monks and nuns and the historic plain people, such as the Amish.

—The desire for health through outdoor exercise and a more wholesome diet.

—The goal of lowering our stress levels through a lowering of ambitions and the envy that keeps us striving to acquire more than our neighbors. We realize that competition may be good for athletic teams, but it is destructive of individual and family.

—The traditional American drive for independence, security, and self-sufficiency. We realize that in this technological world we are all wholly dependent on millions of others for the necessities of life and for our safety.

—The challenge to concentrate on preserving, upbuilding, and renewing the natural resources and human resources around us along with saving from our abundance so as to be able to share the needs of life with those less fortunate, both here and abroad.

—The desire in many Christians affected by the revival of religion in recent years to live more closely by the teachings and example of Jesus, who warned us that we cannot serve God and mammon, that it is foolish to lay up treasures on earth and not be rich toward God, and that we ought not be anxious for tomorrow about food and drink, but about doing the will of God and carrying out His justice in the world.

For some of those who are actively engaged in or wishing to seek a simpler life, there is a heartfelt desire to seek a happy life; one that emphasizes love for persons over material gain. This desire is commendable, but true joy will be found only in communion with Christ that leads on to sharing oneself and one's possessions with others.

The Heavenly Tug

Vernard Eller very clearly points out that the motives for Christian simplicity are positive, responsible urges to show faith in God and love for the neighbor, whereas much of the present-day counterculture, which may also praise simple living and conservation, does so out of negative motives. Secular proponents of a plain life act out of reaction, rebellion, protest, and defiance against society. Christians, from the beginnings of the church, on the other hand, seek out opportunities to serve others.

The warmth that attracts Christians to a plainer life style is that same Spirit which we believe is conforming us more and more into the likeness of Christ. The peace that comes to us when we consciously give up ambitions to be greater than others is the peace of the Spirit. As St. Augustine says in his *Confessions,* ''What do I do when I seek the Lord? I seek a happy life.'' Happiness comes to us when we escape from double-mindedness, trying no longer to live worldly lives and Christlike lives.

Trying to serve two masters is psychologically debilitating because it is frustrating. Such complexity keeps us from simplicity and from peace. As John White observes in *The Golden Cow: Materialism in the Twentieth-Century Church:*

Christians are rarely happy as materialists. Heaven tugs at us too vigorously. We find ourselves apologizing for our new cars or larger houses. This tug of war renders most Christians ill at ease and at times ineffective.

Occasionally you may come across Christians who pursue wealth successfully, yet show no evidence of the struggle. I would say either that their financial success is coincidental, that is to say they find it immaterial whether they make another million dollars or not (for there are some millionaires who do not care a fig for money) or else that their Christian profession is false. In the latter case they experience no heavenly tug in their hearts.

The attraction of adopting a plainer life style to the Christian is thus different from the attraction felt by even the most idealistic secular person. The countercultural person is often an attractive, upright personality, with real feelings for others. Yet his measures for saving and conserving are defensive actions taken against a social and economic order offensive to the radical person. The Christian may not care for these elements in society, either, but he or she stands for Someone, for Christ whom the theologian, Jürgen Moltmann, says becomes oppressed, poor, and even "godforsaken" out of deep love for those excluded from a fully human life. The Christian seeks to save, make do, live without luxury, conserve and renew, so as to share what is saved and protected with others, the brothers and sisters for whom Christ also died.

We must remember that the simpler life we seek is one in which we will decrease so that others can increase—in worldly terms. But more, it is a life style which will lay up our treasure in heaven, not on earth. Only such a Christlike plain life can lead us to final happiness.

Choosing Your New Life Style

John Dewey, the great educator, taught us to think of learning as pupil-centered. Dewey did not play down the importance of content or information, but made it clear that no amount of good advice would do a person any good unless the teacher started out with a knowledge of *who was being taught.*

Throughout this book, mention has been made of the thoughtfulness and care the reader must take in seeking a plainer, alternative life style. No radical proposals recommending adoption of harsh or difficult life styles are made here. For those young enough and tough enough, such life styles are fine. For most of us, there is a limit to the amount of simplicity our age and health will allow. We must aim at modest, moderate alternatives, without continuing to live in luxury and stress, forgetting those who have little of the world's goods.

Thinking of ourselves before we think of things is not really selfish. People deny themselves humanly important experiences in order to support things. We may, for example, decide not to visit our family at Christmas time so as to save the money to apply to a new car. Others may deny themselves needed dental work so as to buy a new refrigerator. We put tangible, hard possessions before human experiences and needs.

Yet, long ago, St. Augustine observed that before we can love our neighbor *as we love ourselves, we must properly love ourselves.* A healthy self-love is the opposite of sinful selfishness, because this love is based on the love which God first gives us. Because we believe God loves us, though we are sinful, we can also love ourselves, as forgiven sinners. We are people of worth, not because of what we do or what we have, but solely because of who we are: children of God.

The attitudinal change needed, then, regardless of the alternative life style we select, must be based on a new assessment of our own humanity and the humanity of others.

When we decide to *love people*—including ourselves—and to *use things,* several elements of the plainer life fall into place. Perhaps, for the first time, we can begin to see the world clearly. We can free ourselves of the fears and anxieties that promote stress in us—and that erode the loving relationships we should have with others.

For example, we can now see that money is not a quality of life; it does not make us what we are, but is only a tool to be used to assist people. Money is a medium of exchange, not a measure of our worth. We may earn it, save it, invest it, spend it, donate it—but only in the way we use a hammer or saw—to accomplish a task that benefits people.

Once people are put first in our lives—because of our love for God, we love the image of God in all others—the things we possess take on a new focus, too. Rather than serving material possessions, as does the person who spends all her time cleaning and improving her house and yard, or the person who constantly washes and waxes his car, we now see things as tools to serve ourselves and others.

Instead of thinking, "I don't want strangers invading the privacy of my beautiful house!" we will think, "I have a lovely home that will give pleasure and rest to someone who needs a place to stay." We begin, now, to see that being rich in possessions is not the real issue. Being rich in sharing, in friendship, is to be rich toward God.

Jesus' great parable of the Last Judgment makes clear that though we are saved by faith, our faith is judged by our works of love (Matt. 25:31-46). As James remarks, "Show me your faith apart from your works, and I by my works will show you my faith" (Jas. 2:18 RSV). Jesus welcomes as the blessed those who visit the sick and imprisoned, feed the hungry, clothe the naked. In loving even the most humble person, Our Lord makes clear that we are loving Him.

The simple life style, then, must include a new allocation of our resources, no matter how great or small they are. We must deemphasize things, stress the conservation of money, and dedicate our money to the service of others. The plainer, simpler life is one of biblical stewardship.

The Elements of a Plainer Life

Peter H. Davids, writing about New Testament foundations for living more simply in the book by the same name offers seven theses summarizing a Christian view of alternative life styles. These theses are worthy of our reflection:

1. All Christian life styles must be Christocentric.
2. A biblical life style will recognize itself as being in opposition to the prevailing values and life styles of our culture. God calls "blessed" whom the world calls "miserable."
3. A biblical life style will be based on the *imitatio Christi*. The Christian life style will be reconciling and peacemaking. (See Matt. 5:9; Jas. 3:17-18.)
4. The focus of the Christian life style will be the worldwide Christian community. It will also be concerned with the needs of those outside the church.
5. A biblical life style will be suspicious of wealth. But suspicion of wealth must mean neither a judgmental attitude nor personal rejection.
6. A biblical life style will be one of sharing with and caring for others.
7. A biblical life style will always stress moderation.

Once the focus of our shift in life style is established, the various elements, or tactics, that we may wish to adopt become clear. Once we concentrate on reducing stress in ourselves, loving people instead of things and sharing with others through gifts and conservation, the following steps seem natural to take.

We will take better care of our own health and that of our family. Pursuing positive wellness, good mental and physical tone, will free us from overusing scarce medical resources; from paying costly medical bills, and will honor our bodies as temples of the Holy Spirit.

Part of this "preventive medicine" discipline will involve reducing and preventing stress, which causes so much disease and unhappiness in our presently "worldly" lives. This will involve reducing dependence upon coffee, alcohol, tobacco, and unneeded drugs. Self-abuse violates the proper self-love that a child of God should have.

We will preserve and improve our health by regular, appropriate exercise. If we are to do more things for ourselves, we will need more energy and physical strength. Strength and a youthful feeling of sufficient energy are possible through watching our diets and exercising regularly. A medical check-up is a must before beginning a diet or starting an exercise program. Jogging or running is a fine exercise but should not be begun without medical advice. Walking has all the virtues of running and may be the exercise for those past middle age.

We will stretch every dollar and use up all the value in every product we have in our homes.

Realizing that the earth's resources are limited and that there are billions of other people to share them, we will waste nothing. We will also study ways to make our buying power greater by purchasing food at "Food Warehouses," shopping sales in supermarkets, using coupons wisely, buying dented cans and generic brands. We will eat day-old bread, which is often sold at bargain prices in stores or special bakery outlets. Otherwise, this food may be destroyed.

We will find ways to "make do" with what we have. We can create logs for our fireplaces by rolling up newspapers. Saving envelopes and mailers can conserve stationery. We can scavenge for dead trees and scrap wood to heat our homes. Goods can be recycled to others at low prices through garage or porch sales. We can buy our reading matter at secondhand paperback book stores.

We can provide some, if not all, of our own food, even in town, by gardening. With a little effort, we can garner healthy exercise and multiply our food budget by raising vegetables in the backyard. Why should all our outdoor efforts go into a lawn? Grass is lovely, but not a necessity. Food is. We may even be able to raise enough food to share with others who are ill or aged. Part of the plainer life is getting closer to the earth itself.

We may even be able to gather wild foods if we study those plants that are safe and tasty. With the exception of mushrooms, which require an expert to differentiate between harmful and harmless varieties, many useful plants may be found on a day's outing in the country.

When I was a boy, at the end of the Great Depression, older ladies used to walk up and down the sides of country roads in the South, picking a "weed" to make "poke salad." I well remember the sight and the taste of the greens.

We can learn again the art of baking at home and save money—while gaining nutrition—in that way. We can use leftovers for casseroles, soups, and stews. We can show unselfishness by not taking more food from the economic system than we really need.

We can live simpler, less expensive lives by learning the basic rules of automotive care and repair. We may be able to do without a car, but many of us will not find that possible. We will still have to travel to work in locales where there is no public transportation. We can form car pools, cutting our motoring costs by $500 a year when we "pool" with two or three others. We can keep our engines in tune and our tires fully inflated, thus increasing the miles per gallon performance of our cars. Changing our oil, recharging our batteries, changing tires—all are possible tasks for most people at great savings.

We may contribute to society by remodeling an older home. In a day of rapidly rising real estate prices, we may find the most economical home is an older one, in need of repair. By learning to "do-it-yourself," we may improve a neighborhood, build substantial equity in a home, and reap much satisfaction. We may even pull our families together as we work to create a finer place to live!

There are many other ways to achieve a happier, plainer life style, but these are the basic elements. Bicycles instead of cars, walking instead of driving, recycling items instead of throwing things away, buying at garage sales, swapping labor with friends, canning food at home, all can constitute the plainer life.

In talking to our friends, we may find that we can learn something useful from almost everyone. Someone at church may know how to preserve food; a Sunday School classmate may help keep our car in shape; the pastor may be able to give information on jogging; a neighbor may know where to buy day-old bread and cakes. Learn the humane art of conversation! *Ask and it shall be given you.*

Look on the bulletin boards at laundromats and supermarkets. Watch the want ads. Write the County Extension Agent. Send for the U.S. Government printing office catalog of useful publications. *Seek and you shall find.*

And concentrate on the main things in life. Seek first the kingdom of God and practice His justice in loving other people. As Vernard Eller says, "All the rest will then be yours." Ask the Lord to give you singleness of mind; purity of heart. *Knock and it shall be opened for you!*

An Achievable Plan

In the April 1979 issue of *Eternity* magazine, there is a remarkable witness to the Christian life style of plainer living. The Lutzes, recently returned missionaries, have decided to continue living a plain life style here at home. Lorry Lutz recognizes the lure of a more comfortable, luxurious life than she had known overseas. Nevertheless, without trying to live as if she were a member of the third world, Lorry wants to live so that she can share both her faith and possessions with all of God's children.

We know that we don't really want to adopt a life style like that of the third world. What we want is a more controlled, plainer life style than most of us live today. Lorry Lutz puts it this way:

> There are many creative ways to develop a simpler life style. My husband and I have also been grappling with this issue since we "re-entered" the American scene. We've had to accept that God has put us back here to live and work in this society. There are uncomfortable tensions when we are out of step with people around

us, especially with our closest friends. Therefore, we are trying to balance our personal needs with the crying needs of a world gone awry, but we must constantly be on guard against being sucked into the mainstream of American life whose goal seems to be epitomized in a best seller's title, *Looking Out for Number One*.

Lorry puts it well. That is the kind of life style that the Christian should find—one that is not "looking out for number one." Yet none of us need adopt the kind of life style Lorry had in Africa—one which was so concerned with just surviving that there was little time left to perform her duties as a missionary.

The Lutzes have worked out some steps that they plan to follow as they bring themselves back in line with American society, without giving in to the materialism that rules so many of us. The Lutzes are aiming at a life style controlled by God and by conscious self-discipline, motivated by a sense of responsibility to the needy world.

Here are some guidelines for the controlled life style the Lutzes have worked out. They are worth keeping firmly in mind:

1. We are trying to stay as close as possible to the kind of life style we had before our income increased—especially in the areas of food, entertainment, and clothing.
2. We are working toward controlling our tastes. We do not need to buy the best, whether in furniture, cars, or any other purchases. When buying our home we decided not to use the maximum loan available to us. Instead we purchased a small, simple home in a respectable, lower middle-class neighborhood. In this way we are able to build some equity for our retirement years without increasing our payments so there is nothing left over to give to others.
3. We are trying to control our credit spending. We have decided to limit ourselves to one major credit card, since it's easier to keep track of expenditures and it limits our credit. Unless we have some emergency, we are determined to pay the full amount at the end of each month to avoid paying finance rates.
4. We also have to keep our mental attitude in check. That means to control feelings of martyrdom or inferiority when visiting others who are living much better than we are. We need to remind

ourselves why we have chosen this life style; and to avoid judging those who have not!

5. We have established a budget which allows us to live comfortably, yet permits the extras that we feel we need from time to time. But the gratifying part of the budget is to be able to set aside more than we ever have before for God's work.

6. Keeping informed of mission needs, conditions, in the third world and relief work are high on our list of priorities. Without conscious attention to the needs of the world, it is easy to become apathetic. We want God to keep us sensitive—and even hurting. Keeping aware of what other people 'have not' helps make us more responsible for what we have.

7. As my husband and I pray together, from time to time we reevaluate our life style, budget, and involvement in missions. We believe that in the three-way relationship of a Christian marriage, disagreement about priorities and expenditures can act as a check and balance in keeping our life style in line with God's design for us.

8. In exposing our guidelines to you, we are putting teeth into them. We need the help of the Body to keep our priorities straight and our controls working.

Mrs. Lutz concludes: "It is still not easy for me to choose to live in less style than others; I would like a bigger, more elaborate house, more fashionable clothes, and all those other things that go along with the marks of success in this society.

"I've not chosen the 'controlled' life style because I like it, but because I believe God does!"

This statement, in essence, is the message of this book. Listen to what the Spirit may be saying to you!

APPENDIX

Mennonite Central Committee List

1. Place ten percent of food-budget money in a designated receptacle as part of Sunday worship experience. Send the money to service and relief agencies.

2. Establish scholarship funds for persons interested in agriculture, nutrition, or community development in needy areas of the world. Encourage people to train for these vocations.

3. Participate in local CROP (Christian Rural Overseas Program) fund-raising activities such as walkathons.

4. Plan with family and friends to give money to hunger programs as an alternative to exchanging Christmas gifts.

5. Fast one day a week or skip the equivalent number of meals.

6. Reduce intake of animal proteins. Most Americans eat twice their Recommended Daily Allowance of protein. Learn how to get more of the protein requirement from plant sources.

7. Reduce intake of sugar and coffee to protect your health, to save money, and to encourage third world countries to use agricultural land for more nutritious food crops.

8. Eliminate highly processed and overpackaged foods from your diet and redevelop a taste for grains (breads and cereals), beans and soybeans, vegetables and fruits.

9. Grow a garden as a family-fellowship project and freeze or can the produce.

10. Buy food directly from those who raise it, if possible.

11. Compost fruit and vegetable peelings and other food residues to enrich the soil near your home.

12. Avoid using commercial fertilizers on lawns or other non-food producing areas.

13. Use part of your own lawn for gardening. Develop community gardens on institutional land. Encourage gardening on school land as an educational project.

14. Ask local public schools to work at the problem of waste in their cafeterias. Challenge administrators not only with the quantity of food wasted, but with values children absorb when they participate in food waste. Visit or write state and national officials (school administrators can tell you whom to contact) and urge them to work at this concern.

15. Work toward removing vending machines with non-nutritious foods from schools, institutions, and businesses. Encourage vending machines or snack bars stocked with more nutritious, low-cost food.

16. Avoid fast-food restaurants where waste of precooked foods and disposable containers is usually heavy, and food is of dubious nutritional value.

17. If possible, carry lunches when you know you must eat away from home.

18. Walk, bike, or use public transportation whenever possible. Carpool when you can. Support public transportation development.

19. Use small cars.

20. Keep track of how much heating fuel, water, and electricity your household uses each month (quantities are listed on utility bills).

Work at reducing the figures whenever possible. Do the same in businesses and institutions if you are in a position to do so.

21. Plan recreation that gives physical exercise and/or builds relationships, but uses little fuel or other nonrenewable resources. Consider hiking, biking, gardening, walking, playing games, visiting, singing, painting, hobbies, and crafts.

22. Find lodging with friends when you're away from home and invite people to use your home. Motels, besides being expensive, tend to put agricultural land on the edge of cities out of production and use vast amounts of resources to build, heat, cool, and otherwise maintain. Camp for the same reasons if you can do it without large investments in equipment.

23. In farming, work at developing production methods that use less energy.

24. Recycle glass, aluminum, and paper, but equally important, use less of those commodities. Ask your community garbage service to provide a recycling system even if it means raising the cost.

25. Use fewer disposables. Examples: carry your own cup instead of using styrofoam throw-a-ways; use cloth diapers except for travel; wipe up spills with rags or sponges. Challenge the trend toward more and more disposables in hospitals and other institutions.

26. Determine to be free from clothing fashions and fads. Learn to live with a smaller, more basic wardrobe. Buy or sew good quality clothing in basic styles and wear garments until they wear out.

27. Mend and reactivate old clothing instead of buying new.

28. Buy used furniture and appliances and reactivate them. Learn to live with fewer appliances and less furniture. Reject fads in home decoration and rely on your own ingenuity.

29. Move into a smaller house or share a large house with more people.

30. Instead of houseware, jewelry, or other selling parties, entertain your friends at quiltings, canning bees, mending parties, breadmaking demonstrations, soap-makings.

31. Stop shopping for recreation. Shopping malls have become our new community centers, built on the foundation of consumerism and affluence. Shop only when you have a list of things that the household really needs. Find more satisfying forms of recreation, other reasons to get out of the house.

32. Buy at small business places where you can develop personal relationships and make your concerns felt. Large chain stores are usually controlled by larger corporations which push growth, more stores, more blacktop, more heating, cooling, and lighting, more land and energy used for consumer enterprises. Small savings one may make in such places are not worth the gas used driving to them and the resources wasted in maintaining them at a growth level.

33. Work to protect agricultural land in your community from being developed for other purposes. Government officials at local and federal levels should be encouraged to support land-use legislation safeguarding productive agricultural acreage from housing and business development.

34. Members of government should be undergirded in efforts to reduce military spending and arms sales to other countries. Urge government to convert weapons research and arms production into agricultural research programs to benefit third world food production.

35. Study the role of "agribusiness" as carried out by corporations both in North America and in underdeveloped countries. Where multinational (agribusiness) corporations have served to widen the disparity between rich and poor and to eliminate small farmers, they must be curbed.

36. Support government food policies committed to world foods security (adequate food aid and a national grain bank) and rural development for small farmers in food-deficit countries.

37. Hunger is still widespread in North America, though it may be hidden from our view. Malnutrition among the elderly, minority groups and the unemployed is particularly common. Find out if there are hungry people living within ten miles of your church. Determine what your church can do to help. Study the problem and the work of existing agencies.

38. See if your church building can be used during the week in a program of mission to the community.

39. Meet as a congregation or in small groups to discuss this list and to add to it. Can you agree on any specific changes people will make and then pledge your support for each other?

BIBLIOGRAPHY

The Simple Life

Cooper, John C. *Finding a Simpler Life*. Philadelphia: Pilgrim Press, 1974.

Dahl, Gordon. *Work, Play, and Worship*. Minneapolis: Augsburg, 1972.

Eller, Vernard. *The Simple Life*. Grand Rapids, Eerdmans, 1973.

Engstrom, Ted W. and Juroe, David J. *The Work Trap*. Old Tappan, N.J.: Revell, 1979.

Foster, Richard J. *Celebration of Discipline*. New York: Harper & Row, 1978.

Longacre, Doris Janzen. *Living More With Less*. Scottdale, PA: Herald Press, 1980.

Nearing, Helen and Scott. *Living the Good Life*. New York: Schocken Books, 1954.

Why Christians Should Live a Simpler Life

Bagdikian, Ben H. *In the Midst of Plenty*. New York: Signet Books, 1964.

De Santa Ana, Julio. *Good News to the Poor*. Maryknoll, N.Y.: Orbis Books, 1979.

Easterday, Kate Cusick. *The Peaceable Kitchen Cookbook*. New York: Paulist Press, 1980.

Finnerty, Adam Daniel. *No More Plastic Jesus*. New York: Orbis Books, 1979.

Goudzwaard, Bob. *Capitalism and Progress*. Grand Rapids, MI: William B. Eerdmans Publishing Co., 1979.

Harrington, Michael. *The Other America*. Baltimore, MD: Penguin Books, 1962.

Keister, John D. and H. Dorothea. *Food, Fuel, and Future*. Philadelphia Parish Life Press, 1978.

Kraybill, Donald B. *The Upside-Down Kingdom*. Scottdale, PA: Herald Press, 1978.

Sider, Ronald J. *Rich Christians In an Age of Hunger*. Downers Grove, IL: InterVarsity Press, 1979.
White, John. *The Golden Cow*. Downers Grove, IL: InterVarsity Press, 1979.

Staying Well

Anderson, George B. and Johnson, Pamela J. *Physical Fitness Digest*. Northfield, IL: DBI Books, 1979.
Ardell, Donald B. *High Level Wellness*. Emmaus, PA: Rodale Press, 1977
Benson, Herbert, MD. *The Relaxation Response*. New York: Avon Books, 1975.
Bolles, Richard N. *The Three Boxes of Life*. Berkeley, CA: Ten Speed Press, 1978.
Breslow, Liri, editor. *How To Get the Best Health Care for Your Money*. Emmaus, PA: Rodale Press, 1979.
Consumer Reports. The Medicine Show. Compiled by the editors of *Consumer Reports*. Mt. Vernon, NY, 1976.
Cooper, John C. *Why We Hurt and Who Can Heal*. Waco, TX: Word Books, 1978.
Di Cyan, Erwin. *Creativity: Road to Self-Discovery*. New York: Jove (HBJ) Books, 1978.
Dychtwald, Ken. *Body-Mind*. New York: Jove (HBJ) Books, 1977.
Garfield, Patricia. *Creative Dreaming*. New York: Ballentine Books, 1974.
Heimlich, Henry J., M.D. *Dr. Heimlich's Home Guide to Emergency Medical Situations*. New York: Simon and Schuster, 1980.
Lamott, Kenneth. *Escape From Stress*. New York: Berkley Medallion, 1975.
Mackenzie, R. Alec. *The Time Trap*. New York: McGraw-Hill Paperback, 1972.
Schutz, William C. *Joy: Expanding Human Awareness*. New York: Grove Press, 1967.
Stein, Jane J. *Making Medical Choices*. Boston: Houghton Mifflin Co., 1978.

Coping With The Middle of Life

Cooper, John Charles. *Religion After Forty*. Philadelphia: Pilgrim Press, 1973.

Cooper, John C. and Wahlberg, Rachel C. *Your Exciting Middle Years*. Waco, TX: Word Books, 1976.

Davitz, Joel and Lois. *Making It: 40 and Beyond*. Minneapolis: Winston Press, 1979.

Hendricks, Jeanne. *Afternoon*. Nashville: Thomas Nelson, 1979.

Levinson, Daniel J. *The Seasons of A Man's Life*. New York: Knopf, 1978.

Sheehy, Gail. *Passages*. New York: Dutton, 1974.

Uris, Auren. *Over Fifty*. Radnor, PA: Chilton Book Co., 1979.

Woodburning and Solar Energy

Bainbridge, David; Corbitt, Judy, and Hofacre, John. *Village Homes' Solar House Designs*. Emmaus, PA: Rodale Press, 1979.

Mazria, Edward. *The Passive Solar Energy Book*. Emmaus, PA: Rodale Press, 1979.

Vivian, John. *The New, Improved Wood Heat*. Emmaus, PA: Rodale Press, 1978.

Saving Money By Building and Repairing Items

Abler, William. *Shop Tactics*. Philadelphia: Running Press, 1976.

Anderson, L. O. and Zornig, Harold F. *Build Your Own Low-Cost Home*. New York: Dover Publications, 1972.

Albright, Robert. *547 Easy Ways To Save Energy in Your Home*. Charlotte, VT: Garden Way Publications.

Bicycling Magazine. *Reconditioning the Bicycle*. By the editors of *Bicycling* Magazine. Emmaus, PA: Rodale Press, 1979.

Blackburn, Graham. *Illustrated Basic Carpentry*. Indianapolis: Bobbs-Merrill.

Braun, Donald R. *Carpeting Simplified*. Briarcliff Manor, NY: Directions Simplified, Inc.

Braun, Donald R. *How To Install Panelling—Valances—Cornices*. Briarcliff Manor, NY: Directions Simplified, Inc.

Cobb, Hubbard H. *Woman's Day Homeowners' Handbook*. New York: Simon and Schuster, 1976.

Cole, John N. and Wing, Charles. *From the Ground UP*. New York: Simon and Schuster, 1976.

Consumer Guide: Fix It. Skokie, IL: Publications International, Ltd.

Daniels, George. *How to Use Hand and Power Tools*. New York: Harper and Row.

Derven, Ronald and Nichols, Carl. *How To Cut Your Energy Bills*. Farmington, MI: Structures Publishing Co.

Hand, Jackson. *How To Do Your Own Painting and Wallpapering*. New York: Harper and Row.

Malis, Gene and Jody. *Workshop Book* (Boy Scouts of America). New York: Berkley Medallion, 1973.

Morrison, James W., editor. *The Complete Energy-Saving Home Improvement Guide*. New York: Acro Publishing Co., Inc.

Organic Gardening and Farming Magazine. The Home Workplace. Compiled by the editors of *Organic Gardening and Farming Magazine*. Emmaus, PA: 1978.

Reader's Digest Complete Do-It-Yourself Manual. Pleasantville, NY: Reader's Digest Association.

Reader's Digest: *Fix It Yourself Manual*. Pleasantville, NY: Reader's Digest Association.

Reschke, Robert C. *Successful Roofing and Siding*. Farmington, MI: Structures Publishing Co.

Sherwood, Gerald E. *How to Select and Renovate an Older House*. Dover Publications, 1976.

U.S. Department of Housing and Urban Development. *How to Insulate Your Home and Save Fuel*. New York: Dover Publications, 1977.

Wagner, Walter F., editor. *Houses Architects Design for Themselves*. New York: McGraw-Hill, 1974.

Wilson, J. Douglas. *Practical House Carpentry*. New York: McGraw-Hill.

XYZ YX Information Corporation. *Home Emergency Repair Book*. New York: McGraw-Hill.

Saving Money and Making Use of Natural Foods

Angier, Bradford, *One Acre and Security*. New York: Vintage Books, 1972.

Consumer Reports: Buying Guide Issue 1980. Mt. Vernon, NY., 1980.

Densmore, Frances. *How Indians Use Wild Plants for Food, Medicine and Crafts*. New York: Dover Publications, 1974.

Gallagher, Neil. *How to Save Money on Almost Everything*. Minneapolis: Bethany Fellowship, 1978.

Gibbons, Euell. "Stalking the West's Wild Foods," *National Geographic*. August, 1973, pp. 186-199.

Gilmore, Melvin R. *Use of Plants by the Indians of the Missouri River Region*. Lincoln: University of Nebraska Press, 1977.

Judd, H. Stanley. *Think Rich*. New York: Dell Publishing Co., 1978.

Kupris, Bronnie Storch. *The Dell Smart Shopping with Coupons and Refunds Book*. New York: Dell Publishing Co., 1980.

Niethammer, Carolyn. *American Indian Food and Lore*. New York: Macmillan Co., 1974.

Phillips, Mike. *A Survival Guide for Tough Times*. Minneapolis: Bethany Fellowship, 1978.

Rodale, J.I, editor. *The Complete Book of Food and Nutrition*. Emmaus, PA: Rodale Books, 1961.

Ruff, Howard J. *How to Prosper During the Coming Bad Years*. New York: Warner Books, 1979.

D. Glen Aitken